REIMAGINING SPIRITUAL FORMATION

REIMAGINING SPIRITUAL FORMATION

A WEEK IN THE LIFE OF AN EXPERIMENTAL CHURCH

Doug Pagitt and the Solomon's Porch Community

www.emergentys.com

WWW.ZONDERVAN.COM

Reimagining Spiritual Formation: A Week in the Life of an Experimental Church
Copyright © 2003 by emergentYS

emergentYS Books, 300 South Pierce Street, El Cajon, CA 92020, are published by
Zondervan, 5300 Patterson Avenue SE, Grand Rapids, MI 49530

Library of Congress Cataloging-in-Publication Data

Pagitt, Doug, 1966-
  Reimagining spiritual formation : a week in the life of an
experimental church / by Doug Pagitt.
      p. cm.
  ISBN 0-310-25687-9 (pbk.)
  1. Spiritual formation. I. Title.
BV4511 .P27 2004
277.76'579--dc22

                                                              2003016095

Web site addresses listed in this book were current at the time of publication. Please
contact Youth Specialties via e-mail (YS@YouthSpecialties.com) to report URLs that
are no longer operational and replacement URLs if available.

Edited by Carla Barnhill and Linnea Lagerquist
Cover design by Dustin Black
Interior design by Burnkit
Printed in the United States of America

03 04 05 06 07 08 09 / DC / 10 9 8 7 6 5 4 3 2 1

917 *

108694

ACKNOWLEDGMENTS

I would like to acknowledge and sincerely thank the many people who have been involved in the creation of this book.

Thank you to my family, Shelley, Michon, Taylor, Ruben, and Chico for your love, patience, and support during my many days away and my paying too much attention to my computer.

Thank you to the beautiful people of Solomon's Porch for helping me to try and live in the rhythm of God. I love you all deeply.

Thank you to Dustin, Erin, Javier and Sarah, and Jim and Carla for sharing your lives through your journals, and to Laura for coordinating the effort.

Thank you to Thom and Carla for helping me write while laughing at and with me all the way through.

Thank you to the authors whose books sell enough to allow books like this to be published.

Thank you to my friends who have helped me attempt to live in community in the way of Jesus: Mark Scandrette, Michael Toy, Holly Zaher, Ivy Beckwith, Tim Keel, Tony Jones, Laci Scott, Brian McLaren, Andrew and Debbie Jones, Tim Conder, Chris Seay, Rudy Carrasco, Brad Cecil, Dieter Zander, Jason Clark, Mark Oestreicher, Darin and Megan Petersen, Rob and Lilly Lewin.

CONTENTS

PROLOGUE

THE STORY OF THE BOOK

Thank you for your interest in this book. Now that it's finished, I know the process of putting all these ideas into written form was worth the struggle—and I can admit it was a struggle.

For one thing, this is not the book I set out to write. I had wanted to tell the story of six communities from the United States and Europe who are exploring ideas about spiritual formation that extend beyond the education model. I would have had each of these churches describe life in its community during a certain week—a "Here's what's happening today in Prague while over in Munich..." kind of thing for which I would be the tour guide. In due course the publisher hinted that my skills were not suited to making that book happen and asked me to tell the story of Solomon's Porch instead.

For another thing, I didn't want to come across like I'm bragging about our church or as though I'm telling people to be more like us. I have no interest in trying to make people think we have it all figured out.

What's more, I'm not a very good writer. I like ideas and I like to talk, but writing is another, more difficult world. In fact, this book exists only because I was able to work in community with others. Thom Olson and I would read the first draft of each chapter together out loud. If we weren't made too queasy by what I wrote, we'd talk about it, sometimes for hours, and then I'd rewrite it. After putting together a version I was reasonably pleased with, I would send the chapter off to Carla Barnhill (who is my friend, as well as part of Solomon's Porch, and was hired by the publisher to edit the book). She would do her magic and send the chapter back. After reading it a few more times out loud, I'd make additional changes, then call it done (until I started obsessing about more possible changes). This went on for four months.

Worst of all was struggling with the concept that ideas about faith and ministry could be turned into a commodity to be sold. The way I see it, God gives people ideas and inspiration for ministry for the benefit of the world. These inspirations are not intellectual property that can then be marketed—they are gifts of God for the Church. Wonderful things happen in the life of Solomon's

Porch and others might benefit from hearing about these things. But by what right do I package them to sell? How dare I make money off the blessings of God?

It took hours of debate and discussion, but eventually my friends in the publishing world helped me understand that what's for sale is not the ideas. All of the ideas in this book are available for free. We discuss many of them on the Solomon's Porch Web site (www.solomonsporch.com), and certainly everyone is free to come and explore our way of living by spending time in our community (okay, you might need a plane ticket, but you get what I mean). But what's for sale is the form. Putting these ideas into properly structured sentences that go into a book that can be delivered to homes or churches or purchased at a bookstore costs money. The hundreds of hours put into this book by all the people involved (authors, editors, printers, marketers, warehouse employees, store clerks, etc.) require that the book be sold at a price.

In other words, the God-inspired components of our community belong to God and are free to all who want them. But if you want those ideas in a format that lets you sit on your own couch while you think them over, you're going to have to pay for it.

Anyway, thank you for buying this book and for spending your time with our community. The truth of the matter is that a book about the life of a group of people will always be a lesser version of the real experience of spending time with those people. So please consider this your invitation to show up on our doorstep and experience life with the people of Solomon's Porch.

INTRODUCTION TO THE JOURNALS

The life of Solomon's Porch is not primarily about the things we do, or the reasons for our doing them. Solomon's Porch is about people. It is a community trying to live with God in the world. So I would like you to meet some of the people of our community, to experience glimpses of their lives.

Throughout each chapter you will meet six people who are part of Solomon's Porch. From January 2003 to April 2003, Erin, Dustin, Jim, Carla, Sarah, and Javier kept journals of their lives and their experiences as part of our community. As you can imagine there was an enormous amount of writing. Laura Towle read every entry and selected a few to include with each chapter. These entries are not intended to be examples of any particular point in the chapter, but are illustrative of the struggle and benefit to life together.

A few hints before you read the journal entries: First, while the entries are not necessarily illustrative of the chapter material, they do at times show wonderful tension. Look for and notice the differences of opinion in the entries and even the material elsewhere in the book. The reality of our spiritual formation is often found in this tension.

Second, each writer has a unique voice. One may write for himself while another writes for the outsider to read. Let each speak in his or her own way, as they all bring unique gifts.

Finally, you will have to determine when to read the entries. They are scattered throughout the chapter, at times in the margins, at other times in the main body. Some have found it best to read the journals first, then the chapter; others go back to the entries after the chapter. Still others read the journals and the main body text together.

Again, thank you for your interest in our book, and welcome to a week in the life of our community.

WE DREAM OF A CHURCH WHERE...

1. We listen to and are obedient to God
2. People who are not Christians become followers of God in the way of Jesus
3. Those who are not involved in church would become an active part of it
4. People are deeply connected to God in all of life; body, mind, soul, and spirit
5. Beauty, art, and creativity are valued, used, and understood as coming from the Creator
6. Culture is met, embraced, and transformed
7. Joy, fun, and excitement are part of our lives
8. The Kingdom of God is increased in real ways in the world
9. The biblical story of God is told and contributed to
10. Biblical justice, mercy, grace, love, and righteousness lead the way
11. Truth, honesty, and health are a way of life
12. We value innovation and are willing to take risks in order to bring glory to God
13. Worship of God is full, vibrant, real, and pleasing to God
14. Faith, hope, and love are the context for all
15. The next generation of leadership is built up and leaders are servants
16. Everyone is equipped to do ministry
17. God's Spirit takes precedence over all structures and systems
18. Christian Community is the attraction to outsiders and the answer to questions of faith
19. People participate in the Kingdom of God in accordance with their abilities and gifts
20. We are connected to, dependent on, and serve the global Church
21. People learn the ways of God and are encouraged to make it central to their lives
22. Other churches are valued and supported
23. People's visions and ideas of ministry come to life

CHAPTER 01

A NEW APPROACH FOR A NEW AGE

Welcome to Solomon's Porch. It is truly an honor to invite you into a week in the life of our community. We hope you will be our guest and find friends and kindred spirits with whom you can journey in the pursuit of life in harmony with God.

Let me make a few clarifications from the beginning. The intention of this book is not to tell you how you can have an effective church in the 21st century. I'm not laying out a how-to guide for reaching "target audiences." I won't even try to convince you that you'd be better off having a church with the practices, intentions, and values of Solomon's Porch. My desire in writing this book is to provide a descriptive glimpse at the efforts of our emerging community on the chance that you will find our story useful as you seek dreams of your own.

This book is more about our community's honest longings and efforts than our accomplishments and results. It is a collection of the hopes and aspirations of a people trying. Our efforts to arrange our lives around communal spiritual formation are, at times, awkward and pathetic. Yet at other times, they are wonderfully forward-leaning and pull us toward God in ways we never anticipated. They are nearly always sincere attempts toward sustainable Christian spiritual formation utilizing practices that extend beyond the education model of Christian discipleship.

Maybe like me you're wondering why I'd write a book when so much of this is in the experimental stage. I've spent many hours struggling with the idea of "selling" what I think of as a vision for Christian community that is God's to give, not mine. What's pulled me through is my belief that there are wonderful people—pastors, teachers, lay leaders, new Christians, lifelong Christians—who are not interested in a model program or approach to spirituality, but are searching the stories of others to find permission to pursue their own deeply held, unspoken intuitions about how faith and church could be. In some ways this book is an act of poetry; it is an attempt to put words around our experiences and desires to allow others to step inside.

DUSTIN BLACK

I think this is where I try to establish my character with some small talk about who I am.

My name is Dustin. I'm the yuppie with a job that allows him to compete in the rat race and grow ulcers at a pace years ahead of his peers.

I'm a 25-year-old art director who dreams of someday owning a monkey.

Snugly raised in south central Nebraska, I graduated from Holdrege High School in May of 1996. I got a degree in advertising and a minor in fine arts from the University of Nebraska in Lincoln and promptly moved to Minnesota.

My parents raised me in a Baptist home, with weekly services mandatory. I was president of my high school youth group for three years. Not necessarily because I

In an ideal world this would be a two-way conversation. We would be mutually inspired by sharing our stories, visiting each other's faith communities, eating in each other's homes, and discovering the details of each other's lives. In reality, of course, we have few options beyond visiting Web sites, reading books, and meeting one another at the occasional "New Church Trends" conference. But I hope that this book will inspire you to seek face-to-face conversations with other searchers as you seek ways to make your own dreams of faith become reality.

JIM BARNHILL

If you need a picture of me in your head, go with a mix of the depressed Charlie Brown, Lucy at her advice kiosk, Linus doing his philosophy, and of course, Snoopy dancing in the Christmas pageant. Then picture this Charlucysnoopynus person holding two children, leaning on my wife, and smiling from ear to ear. That's me, Jim Barnhill.

I'm 35 and the father to my incredibly gifted daughter Emily Rose, age 6, and to my unbelievably good-natured son Isaac, age 2. I've been married to the love of my life, Carla Marie Grover Barnhill, for 10 years.

We're all shaped by our world. The influences in my life include an atheistic best friend who taught me to think and to care for the underdog, an older sister who taught me how to treat women, and living in Christian community.

But the greatest impact in my life has clearly come from living in a dysfunctional family. My parents' conflict-filled relationship created in me both an intense need to understand myself and other's behavior and a powerful, dare I say codependent, need to help people who are hurting emotionally. So the plot of my life seems obvious: having watched two people I love dearly inflict pain on each other for so long, I have devoted my life to healing myself, being the best husband and father I can be, and helping others deal with their own pain. The bummer in all this is that I am often insufferably serious and yet I have the heart of a seven-year-old. Despite my tortured side, I am the most real when I am playing Barbies with my children, arguing with my wife in the form of show tunes, or singing my diaper-changing song to the Music Man tune "Trouble in River City."

In the midst of all this, I have sought desperately for the God who can account for this world of pain and heal it—and, frankly, me too. My upbringing in the United Methodist Church grounded me in the Christian faith, allowed room for doubts, and clearly emphasized that loving others is the way of Jesus Christ. In college, popular beliefs challenged my faith. It was hard to counter my non-Christian friends' charge that "all beliefs are relative." I turned toward evangelical groups that projected a strong sense of confidence, but any doubts I expressed were always brushed off glibly.

I needed answers, so, after leaving UNC-Chapel Hill with a BA in Psychology, I decided to study theology at Fuller Seminary. In seminary, however, I unexpectedly began a spiritual depression: too many different "answers" offered over the centuries to the toughest questions told me that finding the ONE undeniable and indubitable faith was impossible.

Devastated, I decided that I could not serve as a pastor. Since then I have used my pastoral gifts outside of the church in child protection, mentoring programs, and now as a high school special education teacher to students with emotional and behavior disorders.

What saved my faith during this time? A handful of postmodern theologians convinced me that the Christian faith did not need to be justified by "rational" modern scientific criteria to be believable. I came to understand the faith not just as doctrines to be believed but as a way of life to be lived. The all-powerful god who intervenes in the world just for some gave way to the all-loving God who suffers with and for us all.

In Glen Ellyn, Illinois, I began attending St. Barnabas Episcopal Church and learned how high-church liturgical worship can powerfully change us.

Finally, a move to Minnesota led me to Solomon's Porch where I was attracted by its postmodern expression of the faith. So here I am, trying to be faithful, trying to experience the all-loving God that is found in Christian communities who live with and for one another, the God who walks among those who suffer.

I hope something in this book helps you along the way.

A NEW APPROACH FOR A NEW AGE

This book will bring you into our community and our life. You will meet our people through journal entries, hear stories from each day of the week, and be invited behind the scenes to see how we are trying to live. First, though, let me explain what lies behind much of the design and practices of our community. In some ways this book is not about the 21st century, it is about the 1880s and the changes brought by the Industrial Revolution.

Beginning with the Industrial Revolution, innovations in travel, communication, and science have changed the way we define community and live in it. Incredible advances in medicine have made life possible where once there was only death. These shifts have changed the way we think about what it means to share our lives with others and how we measure the value of life. We have revolutionized how we live and nearly all that we believe, know, and understand—but much of the thinking and practices of Christianity have stubbornly stayed the same.

It seems to me that our post-industrial times require us to ask new questions, questions that people 100 years ago would have never thought needed asking. Could it be that our answers will move us to reimagine the way of Christianity in our world? Perhaps we as Christians today are not only to consider what it means to be a 21st century church, but also—and perhaps more importantly—

was the most qualified or most Christ-oriented at the time, but because I felt like I needed to. Couldn't hurt my résumé, right? Plus, my talent for leadership and socialization shouldn't go wasted. Right? It was more motion and less devotion, and in the end I burned myself out and probably some others.

I didn't really attend church in college. It was always something "I'd grow into." My junior and senior year I bounced around a couple of places, but never really found any I connected with. The first time I went to this one church, the pastor used a green crayon to permanently add my name to the quarterly attendance roster. It was like kindergarten all over again, except without recess. Or glue to snack on.

Blah blah blah. Even I'm getting bored typing this

what it means to have a 21st century faith. The answers to all these questions will have an impact on how our faith communities are structured, what we do in those communities, and the practices we utilize for spiritual formation. They bear on how we experience community in daily life, how we relate to others, our faith and beyond, and even how we understand the gospel itself.

Perhaps most importantly for our conversation in this book, these changes call us to rethink the value of the education model in spiritual formation. The heartbeat of our efforts within Solomon's Porch is to pursue a way of life in harmony with God created from means extending far beyond what educational formation can provide. I do not intend to spend time discussing the failings of the education model, but rather to lean into the future with descriptions of our practices, some tried and true, and some experimental.

HOLISTIC FORMATION

One notion we are seeking to reimagine is the whole concept of spiritual formation—how people become Christian and live in faith. In the 19th century it was believed that the most effective way to deepen a person's spiritual life was to increase her knowledge about God. People behaved—and still behave—as though the spiritual part of a person is a separate component that can be worked on and developed in isolation from the rest of the person. This approach has been refined with great fervor over the last 100 years and in some ways has just recently hit its stride.

Our efforts are built upon the assumption that we are able to imagine and create something of greater beauty and usefulness if we move away from speaking of spiritual life in dualistic tones, as if the spiritual part of a person is a separate component that can be worked on and developed in isolation from the rest of the person. We are working with a view of spiritual formation in which we forget about working on a part of a person's life, and instead work with people as if there is no distinction between the spiritual, emotional, physical, social, professional, and private aspects of life. We hope the result of this vision of human formation will be a move toward a place where we focus on the holistic formation of people who are in harmony with God in all arenas of life, and who seek to live in the way of Jesus in every relationship, every situation, every moment.

BUT THEN AGAIN, MAYBE THINGS ARE JUST FINE

There could certainly be an argument made that Christianity is doing fine and that we are not in need of this radical reimagining. It is possible that the way forward centers on the church improving its current approach of education-based spiritual formation. Perhaps all we need is better curriculum and better training for our pastors and teachers. Perhaps we need to make a clearer call for the basics of the faith and be sure that people are well-grounded in their beliefs. Perhaps the church is actually positioned quite well in the post-industrial world and, with some fresh models of teaching and learning, will do just fine.

Perhaps, but I think not, or at least not for us. We join with the many people, professional and lay, who have suggested in writings, conversations, prayers, and pleadings that the Christian Church has not lived up to its potential or calling in the post-industrialized world, but that it could. Maybe there is something to the critique that the church is marginalized in the world to such a degree that the marks of a "successful" church have been reduced to tangible evidence such as size, market share, political influence, healthy budgets, and the creation of model citizens living the American Dream. This marginalization is not due to the Church's poor use of marketing techniques or lack of effort in discipleship. Rather, I've become convinced that our misguided belief that life change can come through proper knowledge acquired through education has failed to produce the kind of radical commitment to life in harmony with God in the way of Jesus that we are called to. When the realities of life crash into our knowledge of God, faith is often the prime casualty. Doesn't the role of communities of faith need to include more than making converts and educating people in right belief? Doesn't it need to also make possible corporate and personal lives lived in harmony with God? I am not suggesting that churches have not sought this holistic approach to faith in other times, but I do believe that the knowledge-based spiritual formation of the 20th century has so reduced the call of Jesus to right belief that many become confused about why mere profession of belief does not bring about life change.

ERIN ANDERSON

Hey, sugar. I'm Erin. Let me tell you a bit about myself. I'm 5'5", 115 lbs., brown hair, hazel eyes. I was born under the sign of Taurus, but I'm more like a Scorpio. I like snuggling by the fire, long walks on the beach, and reading love poetry by candlelight. So now that you know about me, I want to hear about you. Oh, the strong silent type, are you? I guess I'll have to take this bull by the horns and start from the beginning.

I was born into a huge blessed Irish Catholic family in South Dakota. I attended Catholic grade schools. My 4 younger siblings and I were raised by my parents and the dozens of aunts, uncles, and grandparents that lived nearby. After multiple moves, my family settled in St. Cloud, Minnesota, when I was in fourth grade. We attended a stoic German Catholic church. My parents taught confirmation, sang in the choir, and tried to be involved. "Try" was

magazine subscriptions. Newsweek, Dwell, National Geographic Explorer, Blue, Print, Communication Arts, Creativity, Archive and Maxim. Now I have three. Newsweek, Print, and Communication Arts. I get the Star Tribune delivered four times a week and eat Kellogg's Frosted Mini-wheats for breakfast every day. I tried Vanilla Silk for the first time the other day and I liked it.

I never finish a bar of soap. I dated one of the popular cheerleaders in high school and spoke at my high school graduation. That night I got my car stuck in the ditch at the only kegger I went to in high school. I'm on the box of the Daisy 22x BB Gun. You can go to any Wal-Mart and see me hunkered down hunting grizzlies.

For fun I Rollerblade, read, or make out with supermodels.

Okay, just kidding. I can't read. If I had a monkey, I'd train him to sit in the basement and make leather wallets I could sell for huge profit. He'd fling poo at neighborhood children and learn how to tap a keg. I'd name him Scratch.

Well, that's it. That's more than my parents know, and more than many of my friends. Everything I've told you will change in editing anyway. The editor will cut and paste until you go away only knowing that my name is Dustin and I like ponies. But I don't. I hate ponies.

CARLA BARNHILL

The last thing I feel like doing is trying to describe myself. Wait, make that trying to describe myself in a pithy, clever, engaging way so that you'll think I'm at least as creative and funny and brilliant as Dustin and Erin and Jim and Jav and Sarah. There are several things I do reasonably well,

all they could do—many people in the church wouldn't even acknowledge a family that hadn't been coming to the church for 10 years.

Luckily for me, the youth of the church were slightly more accepting. I was very involved in church in high school, one of many reasons why I was labeled a nerd. Other high school activities that pay tribute to my nerdiness: Math League, Future Problem Solving, SADD, Honor Society, band, choir, chamber singers, and orchestra. I was just athletic enough to not get beaten up before I graduated in 1995.

I squandered several years at Concordia College testing out six different majors. (Sorry, Mom and Dad. When I'm a doctor, I'll be able to pay back all the money I wasted tenfold.) I finally chose a major that I could stick to, the Classics (Greek and Latin), after studying in Greece my junior year. After returning from Greece, I transferred to the University of Minnesota. I've lived in Minneapolis ever since.

In college I went to church for various reasons. At Concordia, I got paid to sing in a church choir. In Greece, I wanted to see how culture affected religion. When I got back from Greece, I was agnostic, but still went to church because it felt like it was something I should do. In the spring of 2000, I started going to a church that really changed me, and for the first time, reading the Bible became an integral part of my life. The church didn't turn out to be the right one for me, but it fueled a hunger in me for God that led me to where I am now.

Where am I now? I'm at Dustin's, but I live alone in a studio in Minneapolis owned by my great-uncle. I am a 26-year-old woman who's stumbled upon some good things and is starting to figure out her path. Examples? A few years ago, my uncle asked me to give his two daughters piano lessons. One thing led to another, and now I teach 20 adorable grade school and junior high kids. After I graduated, I got hired through a random headhunter to schedule back surgeries at a doctor's office. Two car accidents and a dozen books about holistic healing later, I'm dedicating my life to the spine—I've decided to become a chiropractor. And finally, a couple of years ago I lived next door to Matt Henry, who introduced me to Solomon's Porch.

I'm warning you ahead of time about my boring journals. My life is so busy that I have little time to interact with people, let alone journal about my interactions. What keeps me busy? Making pies all day. Actually, I divide my energy fairly equally between school and work at the clinic, with a heaping helping of teaching on the side. If that weren't enough scheduled activity, I'm also a hobby queen. I take voice and guitar lessons, and go to yoga class. My super power is underwater somersaults – I can do 14 in a row without coming up for air. I'm not lying. I should contact the Guinness Book of World Records. Did I mention that I'm a nerd?

Well, sugar, if by some chance you're still interested in getting to know each other better, my phone number is secretly hidden on page 347.

A HOLISTIC APPROACH TO COMMUNITY SPIRITUAL FORMATION

In some ways it's a bit odd for a church still in its toddler years to discuss its efforts in spiritual formation. This is particularly true for Solomon's Porch because we are very much in the midst of experimenting with the ideas of this book. My intention here is not to create a plan for others to follow, but to invite people into a needed conversation that will continue for decades. To be honest, the legitimacy of what we're doing at Solomon's Porch will be best judged in 15 to 20 years. In some ways it's easy for people who have chosen our community to live out these desires in the short run at this particular stage in their lives. The question that haunts me is not, "Do people like our church?" but "Is there any real formation happening?" Two decades from now, will our efforts at human formation be shown to have contributed to the lives we have led for the past 20 years? Will they have helped us live as blessings to the world, or will we simply be living the kind of self-absorbed "personal" Christian lives that are so common today?

This is the kind of issue that those who buy in to the educational model of spiritual formation may not need to struggle with. The educational approach provides assurances of effectiveness through tests, catechisms, and statements of faith, which measure whether people have been "properly" formed. When we move beyond belief-based faith to life-lived, holistic faith, the only true test is lives lived over time.

JAVIER SAMPEDRO

This reminds me of my senior English class in high school when we had to write 500-1,000 word essays several times a week. I always wondered if my teacher really took the time to read each paper or if it was just something she glanced over and just gave us credit for. I decided to test this by casually inserting a statement that said something like, "OK, who are we kidding here. We both know you aren't really reading these, but in the event that you are, I will pay you $5." Don't get any crazy ideas. I am not going to test any theories here, because this might escalate into one of those urban legends like the one that tells you Microsoft is testing an email tracking program and will send you money if you forward the message to everyone in your address book 10 times. Needless to say, I don't want to pay what would turn out to be the equivalent of the gross national product of Colombia.

Speaking of Colombia, that is where I was born. Not Columbia the city in South Carolina; Colombia, the country on the northwest corner of South America. So now you know that I am/was an alien, but before you call INS to have me deported for suspected drug trafficking, let me reassure you that I am a naturalized American citizen, and I am only a minor player in the drug industry (more on that later).

but telling people about myself is not even close to being one of them.

I worked at a Bible camp in the summers during college, so I endured more mixers than any human being should have to, but I still can't put myself in a nutshell. I don't have a favorite movie or a favorite candy bar or a favorite color. I can't tell you what kind of animal I'd be or which famous person I'd like to have dinner with. I even have a hard time filling out those e-mail surveys that ask if I eat the stems of broccoli.

It's not that I don't like these games—I enjoy hearing about other people and I yearn to have great answers to these questions so that people will see how truly fascinating and worth knowing I am. But I don't have answers, and that's what makes those games, and this introduction, stressful.

I used to think the problem was that I didn't know myself all that well. But I've come to believe that what really prevents me from describing myself is that people are actually quite complex—far too complex to commit to saying one song or one flavor of ice cream or one bad date defines who we are.

Sometimes when I'm watching Behind the Music or Biography I think about how my story would play out. Maybe a good research team could find deeper meaning in my childhood in a small town in Minnesota as the youngest child of a nice, normal, reasonably functional Lutheran family. Perhaps they would make it clear that my tendency toward people-pleasing is a reaction to my older brother's wayward path. They might even discover the

So my mom decides to bring my sister and me to Miami when my grandparents moved there in 1980. My father stayed in Colombia as he was never really in the picture. I have only talked to him a handful of times in my life. I grew up Catholic as most people in Colombia are, and that didn't change here in the states. I was forced to go to Mass every Sunday. I didn't mind it much most of the time, and I flirted with the idea of becoming a priest. Then came the "P" word that changed all that—puberty. I just could not understand the whole celibacy thing, and there went any more thoughts of the priesthood. I still wanted to be involved in the church, so I did what I could do, and became an altar boy. That experience I think was fantastic, as I was involved in the whole service of the church.

During this time, I was going to a conservative Baptist high school. There I was being taught all about why it was good to be Protestant and not one of those non-Christians who prays to saints and deifies Mary. I started to believe the Protestant theology and eventually left the Catholic church. I continued my involvement in the conservative protestant world by going to a Christian college. My knowledge of God grew almost exponentially. I was doing all the Christian things but still felt restless, like there was more to Christianity than just being up to date on the latest witnessing bracelet.

While in college I started singing in the college choirs and became more involved in music and started writing songs. After four years of playing piano, I moved on to guitar, which is what I play now.

Shortly after college I became more interested in art in general, and how faith and art are sometimes two sides of the same coin. By the time I became a part of Solomon's Porch in the summer of 1999, I had jumped headlong into a new way of thinking about faith and art and how to live each of those out. I don't know if I have learned how it all plays out, but my wife and I (and, by the time you read this, our six-month-old son, Micah) are living a life that promotes both faith and art equally.

The drug industry thing? I work at a treatment center.

By the way, if any of you happen to see Mrs. Whitney, my 12th grade English teacher, ask her how she spent the $5 I had to pay her.

SPIRITUAL FORMATION THROUGH COMMUNITY

There is a call embedded in Christianity that moves us to life together. This idea of holistic spiritual formation is nothing new. In fact, it has a long and prominent history within the Christian church. Throughout history, becoming a follower of Jesus has often meant being brought into a community of people who ate together, lived together, shared their possessions and their lives. We will introduce you to our efforts at being a community of people who not only meet on Sundays, but who become deeply connected to one another. I truly believe that community is where real spiritual formation happens. Most people come to faith not by an isolated effort but through living day by day with people of faith such as their families or friends. People may not fully understand the beliefs involved, but they learn what the Christian life looks like as they see people to whom they are deeply connected living out the disciplines of prayer, worship, and service. Nearly every Christian I know grew into the faith long before they knew a whole lot about it. Even for those who first heard the things of Christianity through an isolated presentation of some sort, this was only the start of a life, not the summation of the life. They were just beginning to understand what this was all about. Isn't this in fact what so many of us still experience—a living of our faith before and beyond our understanding of it?

In many ways, becoming Christian is much like learning our native language; we pick it up when we are immersed in it. I would guess that nearly all of us spoke and communicated long before we started our formal education. What we then learned in school was not the beginning of language use, but the refining of it. In educational settings, the theory of language acquisition through immersion is by far the most successful means of learning. So it is with Christian faith. Rather than seeing Christianity as belief we acquire in a completed form, we ought to enter into it with the understanding that we are at the beginning of a life-long process of discovery and change. Ours is a faith that is lived, from beginning to end.

Community as a means of spiritual formation serves to immerse people in the Christian way of living so that they learn how to be Christian in a life-long process of discovery and change. Christian community can and should be context for evangelism and discipleship, a place where faith is professed and lived.

The word *community* has become the buzzword of the day. Part of the problem with buzzwords is that their overuse can leave them with virtually no meaning at all. In our current vocabulary, *community* can mean everything and nothing at the same time. It can mean people who live on the same street, or people of a similar ethnic background, or people who think the same way about issues. As we of Solomon's Porch understand the term, *Christian community* has four functional elements: **Local, Global, Historical, and Futurical.**

By **local community**, we mean the people with whom we live in physical proximity. It includes the people we live near, work with, drive past, and stand next to in line. It includes those we choose to recognize and those we do not. I find it's often the case that people use the word *community* to refer to those who are most like them. But the story of God from Abraham to Jesus calls us to a deeper understanding of "our neighbor" that embraces those who are not like us at all—and those with whom we worship week by week.

secret of my drive and perfectionism in my need to prove to all those boys who never wanted to date me that they missed out in a big way.

But even the most riveting hour of television would never be able to tell you the truth about my life (or anyone's, for that matter). Any effort to condense all there is to a person into a smattering of anecdotes will not only come up short, it will be riddled with contradictions.

Take me for example: I am a very content woman who is being treated for depression. I have a fantastic husband who I love dearly and fight with often. We are the parents of two exceptional children who I need to get away from regularly. I have a deep faith in God that I question on a daily basis. I work for an international evangelical Christian organization, and the closed-mindedness of the evangelical subculture makes me nutty. I love being home with my children and I miss going to work in an office. I want to contribute my gifts to the life of our community and I don't want anyone to have expectations of me. In the 20 years since I became old enough to vote, I have voted for Ronald Reagan and Bill Clinton.

You couldn't put me in a box if you tried.

I don't say all of this to make myself sound more complicated and intriguing than your average Josephine. I say this because I believe everyone's life plays out in a similar way. We are all bundles of contradictions and conflicting beliefs and ideas.

What has made Solomon's Porch my community is that it welcomes me and my contradictions with open arms. There are people in our com-

Oddly, many Christians find that their fellow congregants play no more crucial a role in their daily lives than the people they walk past in the grocery store. They share a common experience from time to time and receive services from the same organization, but little else. The people of Solomon's Porch seek to make community mean something in our Christian context, so we look for ways to make our community of faith a place where we become involved in one another's lives in intimate, meaningful, transformative ways.

This kind of intimacy requires us to move beyond mere accountability. Accountability is built on the notion that a person will do her own work as she seeks to live a Christian life while others do what they can to keep her on track. This may seem like the best our local community can offer us, but we are striving for more. We feel called to vulnerability. We are seeking to move into relationships where we don't merely ask others to hold us to living in the way of Jesus, but where we invite them to participate in our efforts to do so. We are trying to open our lives up in such a way that others do not simply keep us on track, but become actual agents of redemption and change.

We also understand ourselves as part of a **global community**. We are required to live our local expressions of Christianity in harmony with those around the world. The beliefs and practices of our Western church must never override or negate the equally valid and righteous expressions of faith lived by Christians around the world. It's essential that we recognize our own cultural version of Christianity and make ourselves open to the work of God's hand in the global community of faith.

Christian community also includes those who have come and gone before us, our **historical community**. Just as with local and global communities, there are elements of our historical community that we may well find difficult to stomach, such as the excesses of the Crusades or the Salem witch trials. Though we are not called to live the faith of the past, and we need to be people of faith of our day, our current and future vision for the church cannot be formed without a sense of the visions of the past. It is through our historical community that we are reminded, guided, taught, and led in the ways of God. We are compelled to enter into the context of those who have served, loved, and believed before us. Therefore we must always ground ourselves in the history and traditions of the Christian community that have come before us. There is one body of Christ through all time, and we are part of that body in our particular place and time. If we separate ourselves from the work of our body in previous times, we do so to our limitation and peril.

It's tempting to let our understanding of community end there, but I believe we are called to live in community with those who come after us as well—with our **futurical community**. We owe this concept to a 20-year-old named Luke. During a discussion of part of the Bible that I no longer recall, Luke called us all to a life that is future focused as well as focused on the here and now. He said we are called to live in awareness of the legacy we leave for those who come after us. He said, "What would you call it? Futurical?" And we have ever since.

As we work to create a new way of living in our time, we must also look ahead. Even as we are seeking to create expressions of faith that are meaningful for us in this time and place, we are striving to grow into people who will bless future generations and guide them to do the same for their time and place.

There is something compelling, powerful, and liberating about living life in harmony with God, not in the isolation of an individual relationship but as part of a community that includes those around us, those far from us, those who came before us, and those who will come after us. At the center of this holistic, communal approach to spiritual formation is the creation of Christian communities that are a continuation of the story of God, from Abraham to Jesus to today.

SARAH SAMPEDRO

I grew up on a small farm in southwestern Minnesota. I was the third of six children and always had plenty of playmates. Both of my parents came from farming families in the area so all of my grandparents and most of my cousins lived within a matter of miles. I enjoyed living in the country; it was a very peaceful place to grow up and there was lots of space to wander free. My family was a traditional conservative Baptist family, and we were in church whenever the doors were open. Most of my closest friends growing up were from church because that was where I spent the majority of my free time. Life was good and people were good.

When the time came for me to go to college, I decided to follow my brother who had gone three years earlier to a Baptist General Conference liberal arts school in the Minneapolis/St. Paul area. I had no idea what I wanted to do with my life or what kind of degree to work towards. What I did know, though, was what I liked to do. I liked to create art and I liked Bible/Church history. So, against any better judgment for future jobs, I went ahead with a double major of Studio Art and Biblical/Theological Studies. At the time, I myself did not understand how closely they were actually linked.

During my college years I was privileged to take two amazing trips: a month study tour of Israel and a semester abroad to Italy. Israel was remarkable because there is nothing like visiting the Holy Land. I had only known the biblical history of God through stories but during the trip I got to experience the history of God as tangible reality. My trip to Israel did not affect my life as deeply as my trip to Italy. In Italy, I attended a school not affiliated with my college

munity who hold opinions about war and abortion and art and children and sex and movies that are very different from my own. And what I love is that they have been willing to look beyond my "mom" exterior and the assumptions about who I am that go with it. They have been not only willing, but also eager to jump into the complexity of my life with love and a complete lack of agenda.

I can't tell you how much that means to me.

and became friends with a wider variety of people than I had ever known. I had never encountered people with such different world views. It was an invigorating time in life; I learned and thought and I felt more alive than I ever had.

When I returned from Italy, I no longer felt alive. I struggled to find joy and searched for the cause of my apathy. I still do not fully know why I have felt so empty since I returned. I do know that I had such an amazing experience that breaking away from it caused a depression, and I do know that the friends whom I loved so dearly taught me how to doubt every good thing I had ever known. I learned that life is hard and does not always end perfectly. The American Dream that I had known since birth was not reality.

A dislike for any traditional evangelical church scene followed. It was part of my past that had been an illusion. I could not go to any church for a number of months and I missed being part of a greater whole. A friend mentioned a new place called Solomon's Porch and wanted me to check it out with her. From the very beginning the words and actions resonated with me. Everything that was done was explained; I was told the "why" and not just "this is the way it is done." Every action and experience was intentional and recognized the imperfections of people and life. I could think life sucked and still be in a Christian community.

It is three years later and I still often think life sucks, but I am still in the community. Now I am married to the crazy-haired Colombian guitar player from the church band and we are expecting a baby in a month. The diversity of our histories amazes me and brings me great joy. Life has sometimes been hard for us, but I would not trade my time with him. It was easier for me to live in my American Dream, but the difficulties of love and life have been a much better reality.

THE KINGDOM OF GOD AND TEACHING ABOUT JESUS

It seems to me that this call to communal spiritual formation challenges us to reimagine the gospel itself. Perhaps the challenges of living the dreams of God in the post-industrial world go beyond methodology problems. Perhaps we have been propagating a limited message, reducing biblical authors to sound bytes that cut the gospel message into so many pieces that we are left with little more than statements of what we believe rather than the broader story of how we are to enter into God's story through a life lived in faith.

I readily admit that any attempt to simplify the work of the church over the centuries or the intentions of the apostles of the early church is risky at best. Anyone moving down the road of "summing things up" runs the risk of over-simplification and displaying their ignorance in plain view. With this risk squarely in mind, I contend that Kingdom living and following in the way of Jesus are essential to the way we understand the lessons of the New Testament church. There are many of us who have come to believe that the "gospel" that sits at the center of much of Protestant life today is a bifurcated version of the gospel message, one that reduces the call to Kingdom life to simple belief about Jesus while leaving the exemplary Christian life to the "very" devoted.

Once again, I am not the first person to suggest this. In fact, if you'll allow me to use the following "sound byte" from the end of the New Testament book of Acts, you'll see that these ideas have been present from the beginning of the articulation of the Christian life. The author of the New Testament book of Acts finishes the book by describing the actions of the apostle Paul during his time in Rome at the end of the first century.

For two whole years Paul stayed there in his own rented house and welcomed all who came to see him. Boldly and without hindrance he preached the Kingdom of God and taught about the Lord Jesus Christ. (Acts 28:30-31)

These words offer a needed understanding of the balance between learning about Jesus and living like him.

There is little question in my mind that many of us in the Protestant church have erred in our overemphasis on teaching about Jesus to the exclusion of the call to the Kingdom life. While this is in no way true in every situation, there are far too many times that we allow ourselves to believe that efforts of education about Jesus are the full extent of evangelism and discipleship. This can be seen in the extraordinary efforts around content creation and delivery in churches today.

While the two-handed message of Kingdom life and teaching about Jesus is found throughout the New Testament (and in different forms in the Old Testament), so frequently that I believe that the early church saw these as two inseparably linked pillars of the church they intended to build. In many ways it is hard for me to understand how Christianity became so limited and such a far cry from the Kingdom of God life lived in the way of Jesus.

Perhaps another sound byte would be helpful, this time from the life of Jesus. At the beginning of the Gospel of Mark, the author quotes Jesus at the start of his public ministry saying,

"The time has come," he said. "The Kingdom of God is near. Repent and believe the Good News!" (Mark 1:15)

When I recently "noticed" this passage, it became destabilizing for me. I had always understood the "Good News" as summed up in the life, death, burial, resurrection, ascension, and promised return of Jesus. After reading this almost innocuously short passage, however, I started wondering. What was the "Good News" Jesus was referring to all those years before his death, burial, and resurrection? Could it be that the "Good News" Jesus talked about was less a call to believe in the things that happened to him or would happen to and through him than an invitation into Kingdom life?

At the same time, it is inspiring and even life-giving to imagine an approach to spiritual formation that can impact us in a pervasive, deeply life-altering way. At Solomon's Porch we are seeking a spiritual formation that, in its essence, is not about individual effort but communal action involving a spirituality of physicality, centered on the way we lead our lives, allowing us to be Christian in and with our bodies and not in our minds and hearts only; a spirituality of dialog within communities where the goal is not acquiring knowledge, but spurring one another on to new ways of imagining and learning; a spirituality of hospitality that is not limited to food before or after meetings, but is intended to create an environment of love and connectedness where people are formed and shaped as they serve and are served by one another; a spirituality of the knowledge of God where the Bible is not reduced to a book from which we extract truth, but the Bible is a full, living, and active member of our community that is listened to on all topics of which it speaks; a spirituality of creativity where creative gifts are not used as content support but rather as an invitation for those so inclined to participate in the generative processes of God; a spirituality of service, which is the natural response of all seeking to live in the way of Jesus and is not reserved for the elite of the faith.

Our hope is that this will be evident in a community not limited to supplemental small-group programs but valued as the cultivating force in which lives with God are the claim and invitation to Kingdom life.

So bring your dreams, passions and questions and join us for a week in the life.

At the end of each chapter I would like to share with you a song from our community. This text-only format of music certainly leaves much lacking, but I hope the lyrics will help you catch a bit more of a week in the life of our community.

Selah

Boxed-in savior, My "if then" god.
We've been cheated through Western mind-set.
History is calling, "try to unwrite me."
Flawless, Timeless, Unconfined.

Crooked features
Our systems confine you.
We boast "we're honest 'n willing,"
Yet perplexed and unaware.

When we've tasted
A breath of wisdom,
That's when Wonder should lead us
where…

Chorus:
He's forging crowns of beauty from ashes.
Replacing fear with strength.
Fashioning gladness from mourning.
Mmm, peace for despair.
Mmm, peace for despair.
Mastering mercy, driven by process.
Delivering wellness with a latex hand.
Serviced on Sundays
With a side dish of music.
Looking for freedom
And a one-night stand.

Wonderful God of Israel.
Isaiah, you've foretold.
We have been unfaithful.
Wondering why we're told
that you're…

Chorus:
Forging crowns of beauty from ashes.
Replacing fear with strength.
Fashioning gladness from mourning.
Mmm, peace for despair.
Mmm, peace for despair.

Help us forge crowns of beauty from ashes.
We're called to replace fear with strength.
Fashion gladness from mourning.
Bring, peace for despair.
Mmm, peace for despair.

CHAPTER 02

AN UNCERTAIN FUTURE

Our attempt at being a church began in January 2000 in a small second-floor loft space in a hip little neighborhood of Minneapolis called Linden Hills. The church was actually birthed much earlier, from conversations between a few friends who shared a desire to be part of a community of faith that not only had a new way of functioning but also generated a different outcome. At that point I had said, on more than one occasion, that I didn't think I would be able to stay Christian in any useful sense over the next 50 years if I continued with the expression of Christianity I was currently living—pretty disconcerting stuff for a pastor. This was not a crisis of faith in the typical sense; I never doubted God, Jesus, or the Christian faith. And yet I had a deep sense, which has actually grown deeper since, that I needed to move into a Christianity that somehow fit better with the world I lived in and not an expression reconstituted from another time.

Let me start with my own story. My religious training and experience is from the evangelical stream of Christianity. I came to Christian faith as a high school junior, and immediately I was a leader within the high school ministry of Campus Crusade for Christ. I began attending churches right from the start and was engaged in ministry and Christian witness. Within a decade I had graduated from seminary and experienced 10 wonderful years as a youth pastor at a nationally recognized megachurch. I was even a frequent speaker at regional and national youth events. My world wasn't crashing down. I wasn't at a moral crossroads; I hadn't hit rock bottom. There was no big dramatic shift in my thinking but rather this lurking sense that there were levels of faith I knew nothing of and yet needed to enter if I was to remain a Christian at all. It was a feeling I couldn't shake, and yet I also felt like I couldn't fully articulate what I needed. I just knew I needed something to change.

When I shared this nagging sense of discontent with a few others, I found they were feeling a similar desire for expressions of faith built around new forms and new outcomes. Together we decided to try to organize our lives around a way of living life in harmony with God. (While this might sound very grandiose, it was really more of a pathetic, groping attempt not to discover something beyond Christianity, but to live in the very Christianity that had captivated us in the first place.)

ERIN
2 March, 2003

I began the day with my first prayer partner meeting. Katherine and I went to Laura's apartment. I was pleased to find that the three of us had a strong connection, support for each other, and good ideas for our church and for the world around us. I look forward to seeing how the power of prayer for each other and sisterhood will ameliorate our lives.

I've gone into this church experience being very wary toward church communities, but my mind has been changed person by person. I not only trust the people at church, but I feel more and more drawn to them. I never thought I would let myself get so involved emotionally or socially in a church.

I have no regrets over my experience within the evangelical faith community. I will be ever grateful to the institutions and people who invested so much in me, yet my life experiences have lead me to desire ways of Christianity beyond the practices and beliefs of my beginning. I began wondering if my experience as an evangelical was a great place for me to start but not a sufficient place for me to finish. Solomon's Porch was fueled by a desire to find a new way of life with Jesus, in community with others, that honored my past and moved boldly into the future.

A USEFUL RELIGION

After coming to faith at age 16 from a background with no church involvement, I found myself on a crash course of indoctrination into Christianity. During the early years of my faith, I was surrounded by wonderful people who taught me about the Bible, life, and faith. In the circles I ran in, short summations of Christianity were very much in vogue. One of the most common was, "Christianity is not a religion, but a relationship with God." There was something appealing about this kind of tidy definition that was meant to make faith more than a meaningless ritual. But over time it began feeling like code for allowing my life to be limited to self-indulgent efforts centered on a personal relationship with God with little regard for faith's public usefulness to others.

So I began asking questions of my life and faith that were not centered on how deep my faith was, but how useful was my life in bringing about the things of the kingdom of God? Being a properly trained evangelical, I began scouring the Bible to find the impetus for a life that was good for the entire world. From those years of inquiry comes much of the thinking behind Solomon's Porch—and hence this book. This phrase from the book of James was especially meaningful:

> *Religion that God our Father accepts as pure and faultless is this: to look after orphans and widows in their distress and to keep oneself from being polluted by the world.* (James 1:27)

As we started forming the practices that would become Solomon's Porch, this verse helped to set us on a path of becoming people who are concerned with more than our own salvation—people bent on practicing a Christian faith that is useful in the world.

THE NON-ANTI APPROACH

Please don't assume that Solomon's Porch comes out of a reaction to the evangelical approach. In truth, we never set out to be *anti-* anything. Instead, we long to bring the best of what we have experienced with us and use it to help us move toward a new way of life. This desire to step into the present with a grateful attitude toward the past and a mandate to generate a way of life sustainable for the future is at the heart of our intentions.

So if we're not *anti*, who are we? I've actually become fond of the prefix *post* to describe who we are seeking to be. *Post* does not mean "against" but "after," as in *post*-game report or *post*-war era. In this sense our community might well be described as *post-evangelical, post-liberal, post-industrialized*, and for that matter, *post-Protestant*.

By *post-Protestant* I certainly don't mean *anti-Protestant*. The Protestant church is the Reformation church. When Martin Luther saw that practices in the church of his day had outlived their usefulness, he felt a calling to revive the faith—not to abandon everything that had gone before but to recover the dynamic elements of the gospel. We today have the same calling. We can best honor the reformers of all the ages by doing as they did and not just parroting what they said. We can and should be always re-forming—always seeking to create new ways of life and new ideas about theology, service, and love that are fitting for our world and our time.

Yet from its beginning the Protestant church has tended to define itself by what it is in opposition to. It's essential to realize that a new expression of Christianity can be born out of a desire to build on the past and not simply repudiate it. Without capitulating to the whims of the day, we can pursue common connection with all activities of God wherever and in whomever they are found. We are free to and called to allow our communities to do what Christians have done throughout the ages: to allow Christian faith to come to life in our world.

I recognize that today's "post" is tomorrow's "passé," and I'm okay with that. I certainly don't think the reformers intended for their ideas about the church to be its final form for all time. Similarly, in our time we are called to make our contributions in the world a blessing for those around us and for those who follow—but it's not our job to create all the processes and patterns of the future nor "the thing" for all ages. Future generations will contend with the legacy we leave them—but I certainly don't want to burden my children with an expression of

March 7, 2003
I realize what a balancing act my life has become lately. School, work, lessons; old and new friends; physical, spiritual, and emotional health; hobbies. It seems like I focus my attention on one thing, then realize how neglected another part of my life is, which distracts me from something else I need to do. I pray that I am able to incorporate all things fully into my life holistically rather than in compartments. I also need to pray that God shows me what parts of my life really deserve the most attention.

Today, I received a letter of acceptance from Northwestern Health Sciences School of Chiropractic. I wish I could start tomorrow. For the first time in my life, I have no reservations about starting a program. It is so

comforting to have a path that God has made clear to me, and that I am ready to follow. I am so excited about chiropractic, partly because I just really would like to help people who are in pain, and also because I really would like to educate my patients about holism and the body/mind/spirit connection.

JIM
11/02

Our first meeting with the new small group has taken place, and it seems as though we've cast our lots. There's no going back now. When we decided to do this, it meant that we were going to be committed to these folks, no matter who they were, and begin loving them. There are so many beautiful things that can and will come about by this kind of community. Emily feels com-

faith that fits my time but won't fit theirs. My hope is that what we do today at Solomon's Porch will inspire future generations to dream their own dreams and give life to their own visions rather than feeling the pressure to implement ours.

SERVICED ON SUNDAYS

In the early days as we shared our desires for the feel, intentions, and ways of Solomon's Porch, we often asked a key question of one another: "What in your past that was lifegiving could we incorporate into our lives together?" We didn't have a predetermined picture of how we wanted this experiment to unfold; we were seeking something new, together. We didn't look at handbooks or guides to starting a church. We had no interest in doing a "cover" version of someone else's church model. We knew there were aspects of our pasts that were useful, beautiful, and could benefit others, and we knew there were still other aspects of faith we had little or no exposure to. From these discussions came the basic elements of our community, and we have sought to continue this invitational creative process over the last four years. We often say that we want the dreams of Solomon's Porch to reflect the dreams of the people in our community (see p. 17). We want that list to keep growing and changing with us. It was never meant to be stagnant.

This idea of bringing our dreams to the church is quite different from the model of the "program" church many of us had experienced where the community becomes a collection of services meant to meet the felt needs of the congregants. We never wanted Solomon's Porch to be a place where people were "serviced." A few years before the start of Solomon's Porch, my wife, Shelley, and I were visiting a church that met in a school cafeteria. We sat in the back, and there was a couple sitting in front of us. While we never actually met them we did feel a strange connection with them after staring at the backs of their heads for an hour. As the service ended the husband turned to his wife and in the midst of a yawning stretch said, "Well, that wasn't so bad."

That's the kind of thing I say when I get up from the chiropractor's table or when I get my oil changed in less than 30 minutes. At that moment I knew that if Solomon's Porch—just an idea at the time—ever happened, I didn't want it to become a provider of religious goods and services, no matter how hip they were. I believed the church could be more, that it was reasonable to hope for a deeper response than, "That wasn't so bad." From the beginning of Solomon's Porch, we have referred to our time together on Sundays as gatherings and not services. It's a little thing, but it reminds us that we are here to live life together, not simply have our individual needs serviced.

SARAH

4/15/03

Today I've come to one of my favorite places – Pacem in Terris – Peace on Earth. It's located near a town called St. Francis – very fitting. Anyway, I'm here and I love it. It seems like the first thing that happens to me every time I come is that I sit down and tears just start flowing. Tears of stress, tears of relief, tears of longing – everything seems to let loose in that one moment and I begin my time of solitude less burdened. I've been sitting here quite awhile and all these things keep flooding into my head that I would like resolved. Most of them are questions of God or issues/burdens in my life that I would like to come to terms with. I'm only going to be here for one day this time, so that's not much time for me to ponder my questions of life. I'm hoping that it will be a beginning, though.

-How to deal with having a baby and how to raise him to best love God and live Christianly; how to help him be healthy and what his name will be. I pray that he grows in wisdom and stature with the Lord.

-What Javier and I should do about jobs; that we will be taken care of financially

-Why have I been so angry and easily irritated for the last few years; why my life has been so unsettled?

-Should I get a mentor?

-What kind of woman do I want to be? I need a niche; a place where I know my gifts and know how to use them.

4/16/03

I've been sitting in my hermitage all morning. Just sitting. Well, I was reading and praying, too, but I have been here for hours and it feels wonderful.

　　Answers I have been seeking…

-Mentor? A name has come to my mind.

-My niche? Promote the arts more; provide some leadership there. I love to bake but don't want to be Suzy Homemaker; I could never be a super hostess like some other women in our church, but I enjoy baking but shouldn't eat all the sweets and Javier doesn't really eat them all that much. So, I could bake for the church gatherings. In a funny way, baking is a way that I show love to people; I like them to feel happy and satisfied (like I do) when they eat yummy things.

-Anger? I haven't been peaceful about God's promises. I've lost sight of them, as demonstrated in what I quoted from The Myth of Certainty.

pletely comfortable around adults and gets so much from their presence in her life. Chief among these things is the fact that she understands that all of these adults are people who can lead her, people who she is to listen to. But they are not there simply as authority figures; they show her how beautiful and creative she is. They laugh with her, sing with her, indulge her in her millionth "pretend I'm the mommy" act. From this community and from others she's been a part of, she and now Isaac are seeing themselves as the gifts of God that they are. They are also seeing that our family is not the end goal of their lives. By being a part of this Christian community, they see a constant example of how we serve one another, of how Christians drop what we are doing to meet the needs of a person, of how we take care of one another when we need encouragement. They are seeing how to love others and how to receive love as a gift. What better could they get from any church experience? This community is forming them into people who know the truth because they are living it.

CARLA
2/9/03

To me, the things Solomon's Porch is about are things that are hard to get our heads around. Ironically, that's particularly true for those of us who come from church backgrounds. I think that the people who grew up in the evangelical culture wait for the words they're used to hearing—sin, repentance, salvation, evangelism—in the context they're used to—altar calls, presen-

There are many more things that will develop from all of this, I'm sure. These are just a few of the simple answers I've gotten for now. I'm feeling the urge to get moving again and be active for the day. Above all, I need peace. I need to remember how to rest in that peace and not let my life overwhelm me.

4/16 night

I always forget how hard reentry is when I've been in solitude. Even driving back into the city is difficult. The traffic and rush of people press in on me, and I feel like I'm going to suffocate. All of the things I need and want to do come flooding back to my mind, pushing out the peace that I so joyfully rested in. It's so much easier for me to be with God there. I am much too easily distracted here. I think I miss him the most when I come back, even though I should be able to "bring him with me." I feel like as soon as I get in my car and start driving, I'm moving back away from him and away from peace. Back to the hustle and bustle and overwhelmingness of life. Oh, how I miss him. My heart longs for him. Perhaps this is my little glimpse of Heaven on earth.

NO GUNS, PLEASE – TARGET-FREE ZONE

One of the occupational hazards of pastoring our new community is having to justify its existence. I wish I could count the times that churchly insiders have asked, "So who are you targeting? What demographic market are you going after?" I usually attempt to deflect the questions to hide my disgust. It seems to me that targeting is done by tobacco companies and snipers, and the one who is targeted is rarely appreciative.

The assumption behind these questions is that everything is a product that can be marketed, sold, and consumed to meet needs—everything, including Christianity. Comodification of Christianity may be among the greatest threats to living a viable Christian faith that we face in our world. This assumption is in serious need of rethinking. Unfortunately much more energy has gone into discovering the best use of marketing techniques for the church than reflecting on what happens to the gospel when it becomes a product of an ever-desiring culture looking for "value-added" faith as the final rung of the self-actualization ladder.

During the early days, it would not be uncommon for a passerby to notice us working on our meeting space and ask, "What are you doing?"

"Well, we're starting a church," I'd say, hoping they'd ask when they could start coming.

Instead the typical response was, "Starting a church? What are you doing that for? Aren't there enough churches already?"

Now that kind of interaction can take the wind right out of any upbeat church-starter's sails. Finding a legitimate response for those questions—not to mention my own conscience—became serious business. After months of discussing the integrity of our intentions as a group, we realized that we started Solomon's Porch not because the pews in other churches were full, but because the places of dream making and leadership in other churches were full. There were too many existing communities of faith in which outsiders simply hear words about God packaged in attractive and relevant ways and too few places in which all could participate and experience the transformative workings of God through community. Our desire was to create a place where those who are envisioning new ways of Christianity could give birth to their dreams together. This convoluted explanation may not have been sufficient for the cynic on the street, but sure proved useful for us in understanding who we were becoming.

When we started the church I wanted to begin the practice of journaling. In an effort to remind myself that this was important, I bought an expensive journal, the really nice kind—brown leather binding, gilt-edged leaves and all. In fact, it looked more like a Bible than a journal. (I had visions of my great-grand-children finding the journal and reading about the spiritual development of their deeply reflective great-grandfather at the turn of the 21st century.) I began with high hopes that journaling would make me that "spiritual" person.

In April of 2002, as we started packing to move to a new space in a different neighborhood, I stumbled across my journal. I opened it, expecting to find the heartbeat of where we were in the early days and how this move was part of our unfolding story. What I discovered was that I'd only made two entries, one on the day we signed the lease in July 1999, and the other on January 5, 2000, three days after our first worship gathering.

As disappointing as it was to see my miserable failure at journaling right there in a lack of black and white, there was one noteworthy entry. (In retrospect I figure that's 50 percent useful material—actually not bad for a beginner.) It reminded me how interested we were in being a community of people living in the way of Jesus and how uninterested we were in targeting people for the purpose of church growth.

tations of the gospel. But in waiting for the forms, it's easy to miss the presence of all of those essential ideas.

I feel like we touch others and draw them to Christ by showing them what it means to live as Christians. I just feel like dogma never works, like people are hungry to see a better life, a better way of dealing with the difficulties of life and that I can show them that by the way I live and make decisions and treat people.

I was also struck by something I had sensed, but not really thought about before. I don't think I've ever been in a place with so many openly broken people. I think of any church or Christian community I've even been in, the people at Solomon's Porch seem more aware *of sin and suffering because so many of us have experienced the devastation of sin— divorce, depression, sexual abuse, chemical abuse. If anything, we seem to be a group of people who are acutely aware of our need for salvation, our complete dependence on Christ. I think it's incredibly short-sighted to say that sin isn't talked about at our gatherings. It's not only talked about, it's what brings us together. Jimmy and I are there because we can be open about our failings, about our doubts and questions, about our struggles. But we are also there because we want to be part of a community of people seeking to make our faith, our salvation, mean something beyond our own redemption. We want our faith to matter in the world.*

January 5, 2000:

It is now January 5, 2000. I have done a terrible job of journaling. I don't know why it is so hard for me to journal. It may be the drain that it is for me to write, or it may be that I fear introspection.

We had our first worship gathering on Sunday, January 2nd. It was great. K.P. told her story using poetry and Psalms. The guys did all of our own music. Lord, thank you for letting that dream come true for us to do our own music. Michelle is starting work on the prayer room and gallery today. Andrea is coming in to talk about poetry. It has been really good having this space to create in. There were more than 100 people at our gathering and a bunch from the neighborhood. I am nervous that people in the neighborhood will not understand or like what we are doing. I need to and want to trust that we can simply be us and allow the Spirit to do the rest. The pressure to grow is already mounting and I don't like it. Jesus, we have prayed and said that we want this to be your place where you lead and create us into a community of faith, so again, I tell you that we will follow.

From the beginning we sought a relationship with the world that is not based on marketing or hunting metaphors. We did not start with the idea that we had a corner on the market of God or had a product of faith that we could deliver to our target audience more effectively than other churches could. We never intended Solomon's Porch to be specially formulated to meet the needs of Generation Whatever. Sure we're a young community, but our attention is not focused on a demographic approach of meeting the felt needs of the coffee-house-visiting, cell-phoning, shuttle-disaster-watching, Jetta-driving, Internet-addicted, body-pierced children of the "me" generation that so many of us are.

The efforts of Solomon's Porch began, and remain, our attempt to be people of useful faith—a blessing to the world. Our practices are genuine expressions of our collective community, not marketing tricks. At first glance, some of our ways might seem trendy and many of them will likely change as our community changes, but we are not trying to be culturally chic. We are trying to live a life that is candid and authentic. We are not interested in living a fulfilled version of our current lives, we are seeking to become something else, something more.

DUSTIN

*Tonight I skip working out and Ad league bowling to attend church Bible study. Oh, whoops,
Bible discussion group. If Doug saw me make that slip, he'd fo' sure throw me a beat'n. Getting
the right name to everything at church is an art form. And mistakes only bring swift vengeance.*

Dustin: "So I really liked the introspective prayer at the church service last night... "

*Other more devoted church person smacks me upside the head, juts her hip out and wags
a finger: "No you didn't. No, you did not just call our church gathering a church service.
Shizzam D, I best be kick'n you fo' that."*

D: "I'm so sorry, I just haven't been a member long enough to—a"

*Other: "No you didn't. No, you did not just call your peeps members. We are participants.
Shizzam dawg. I oughtta rough you up right here."*

---

*Time slipped by without much notice, and before I knew it, it was too late to make it back to
go to church. I wouldn't have ordinarily thought too much about it, but for several weeks now I
have been reading the announcements. At the end of the service when everyone is tired of
sitting and they just want to go eat, I pop up and read off a screen about upcoming events at
the Porch. Sometimes I try to break up the horrible boredom I sense in others by tossing in a
couple "jokes."*

*If I can just put one smile on someone's face the last five minutes of worship, I feel I've
done my part. Yet tonight I won't be there. And chances are, no one else will be able to read
off the screen. Surely the church will be ripped apart. Children will run crying to their mothers,
families will disown their kin, and women will tear their robes in anguish.*

*OK, I'm sure no one noticed, but I felt bad for ditching. Next time I set up a climbing trip
with three random strangers, I'm going to be gosh-darned sure I'm back at a reasonable hour.
(Mom and Dad, when I say "reasonable hour" I mean "the bail bond man showed up.")*

Sunday, March 3

*I leave work in time to make it to church by 5:30 and find a place on one of the low-riding
couches. Finding the perfect seat is so essential to worship. Get in a too low couch and your
back starts to hurt. Get too close to the front and you might get called on. Sit too close to the
kids and their chatter pierces through the sermon. Sit in a chair and look unapproachable and
lonely. Sit in a big couch alone and look like a leper or unclean. Sit with the regular group and
look antisocial, and sit with a stranger and risk looking like the creepy church guy coming on
too strong. Think about it too long and look like an arrogant idiot that isn't spontaneous
enough to just sit down. Man. Church can be so hard.*

ADOPTED CHILDREN

We have never been satisfied with people looking over our community to decide whether we have the "right" emphasis, core values, or programs to fit them. Rather, we ask people to bring to our community their contributions and by their involvement to help us be more life-giving. I look at this in much the same way that Shelley and I and our children, Michon and Taylor, approached the adoption of our two younger sons, who had lived next door in a foster home. We did not present Ruben and Chico with a list of the kinds of things our family likes to do and a directive to get in line with it. We invited them into our family, showed them what was important to us, and asked them to add to our family with their lives. We did not just become a family with two more people in it; we became a new family.

So it goes with Solomon's Porch. When new people join us, we become a new community. We ask them to contribute and lead us in new ways. This undoubtedly adds a level of structural difficulty, but so far it's been well worth the effort.

It might sound like I am suggesting that we really know what we're doing. But the truth is we are a community making up the answers as we go along. We are a community brought together more by asking similar deep-seated questions than by all having the same answers. Though answers are useful, we desire not simply to apply the well-grounded answers to previous question, but to be captured by the pursuit of new wonderings.

In July 2002 we took a journey and relocated four miles east to a really great "underprivileged," heavily social-serviced neighborhood called Phillips. From hip to needy—what a wonderfully forming move in location this has been for us. We hope that the same transition takes place in us so that we live as a people needy of the Kingdom of God rather than as a hip people who have something to prove.

Subjects of Change

On my own I've defined.
All that's gathered, all that's mine.
Can we chase it? Will we find
Something sacred, more divine?

Pre-chorus:
I give my mind, each notion.
I give my heart, it's broken.
You gave your life, a token for...

Heavy shoulders search for light.
Growing colder, looming fight.
Apprehension, must all die?
Waiting is over, yours not mine.

Pre-chorus

Chorus:
This will of mine.
With pride will stain.
God's way and God's time.
We're subjects of change.

Foolery's over . The game is done.
Passion playing, God's own Son.
Misty garden, pleading One.
Willing servant, sin undone.

Bridge:
Following the King of Kings.
We will see angel wings around us.
So constantly we must sing.

CHAPTER 03

SPIRITUAL FORMATION THROUGH WORSHIP

SUNDAY

The Sunday night before writing this chapter, I was sitting next to Shawn, who has been part of Solomon's Porch from the early days. We were 15 minutes or so into our worship gathering when a young woman who I hadn't seen before walked through the doorway into our worship space. She stopped and stared. Just then she was greeted by someone near the door who was giving "the lay of the land." I could tell she wasn't sure if she was excited or confused. I leaned over to Shawn and said, "Even after three years it still cracks me up to see the look on people's faces when they come in here for the first time."

It is quite a feat for people just to get to our space. We meet on the second floor of a renovated office center built in the 1930s in an underprivileged neighborhood of Minneapolis. The building doesn't look anything like a church, even when you walk in the door.

On the lower level there is a lobby, kitchen, and an art gallery space. We try to have someone at the door to welcome people and assure them that they've come to the right place. Guests are then invited to proceed up the stairs to the main gathering space where a second greeter waits to meet them. When people walk into the room, they are often so taken with the oddity of the space that much of what the greeter says goes right by them.

The door is on the long end of the 4,000-square-foot rectangular room. The walls are multicolored and decorated with paintings, photographs, and sculpture. Tables are covered with candles and communion elements. People expecting rows of folding chairs find instead groupings of couches, chairs, end tables, recliners, and the like arranged in the round with an open center area. The musicians are located across from the door, but not in the center. Projector screens adorn the corners of both long ends of the room so people can see a screen no matter which direction they face. Because we meet in the round, some people are facing the door, and others are looking away from it.

The greeter at the top of the stairs will point out the bathrooms, the food table, and available places to sit. But the greeter's real job is to assure our first-timers that it's okay if they're late, it's okay if they aren't sure where to go next, and it's okay if they just want to grab a chair in the back corner of the room until they get the hang of things.

While the look of a first-timer still makes me smile, I find even greater joy when I see that person bobbing their head to a song they've never heard before, or joining us in a posture of prayer, or making their way to a communion station to grab a handful of bread and a cup of juice. I love watching people melt into our community and join us in the practice of worship.

WORSHIP AS SPIRITUAL FORMATION

Our Sunday night gatherings officially start at 5:30 p.m., so people are sometimes puzzled when the music doesn't start until 5:40. At least once a month someone asks me, "Why do we start late?" I tell them we aren't starting late, we're starting with conversation. And that's important because this conversation is the heart of who we are. Our hope is that the music, the invocation, the prayers, and the sermon that follows will be a continuation of the conversation between us and with God.

The worship gatherings are certainly the high point of our community life for many of us. But they are not the sum total of who we are or what we strive to be. Instead, we think of our Sunday gatherings as a microcosm of the community we are trying to become. What happens on Sunday night plays out in other times and places in our community during the week, and what happens during the week is incorporated into our gatherings. Our worship gatherings are a reflection of us as a community. It is in the gathering that we learn the language of our community, where we regroup to practice the particular habits and patterns of the faith we're trying to live. Our efforts at Wednesday-night hospitality or Saturday-afternoon service would quickly dry up if we weren't intentional about practicing those efforts on Sunday nights as well.

We're big on words and their meanings at Solomon's Porch, so it's no small thing to us that our time together is called a worship gathering. Both elements, the worship and the gathering, hold sway here. Our gatherings are about God. Because we believe God is to be the center of life and that God adds texture, taste, and depth to life, we gather to learn, experience, and share God in many of the ways Christians have for thousands of years.

We include an invocation early in each gathering as a way of communally acknowledging the presence of God in our midst. There is no soft pedaling here. The invocation will often state clearly that we believe Jesus is the Son of God and that we worship Jesus as the Lord and Savior of all. And yet we seek to do more than simply worship Jesus or hear the teachings of Jesus or gather in the name of Jesus. Our desire is to arrange our lives to follow God in the way of Jesus.

Our intention is that Sunday-night gatherings be a time when people contribute to the creation of a setting in which we are transformed, not a setting in which people come to be serviced by professionals or qualified volunteers. I like to think of it as having dinner at a friend's house where it is expected that you will help pass the serving dishes and clear the table at the end of the meal.

Our gatherings reflect our belief that we are in this together and that we all have something to offer here. Our worship gatherings are not meant to be shows or concerts. They are designed as interactive experiences. We invite participants to join in, share what they have, and take a piece of what those around have to give. We are a gathering of people who are on a pilgrimage through life with each other and with God. Our gatherings for worship are designed to help us along on that journey.

I often wonder if my deep belief that we cannot live in harmony with God outside of a Christian community is driven by my early years as a Christian. When I was 17 years old and a new Christian, I was unaware of the extensive Christian community around me. One day I was driving in my Toyota Corolla thinking about how few Christians I knew and how hard it was to follow Jesus alone. I was listening to a Keith Green tape I'd purchased during my first-ever visit to a Christian bookstore. (How 1983 is that? And no, I didn't have a mullet.) I remember being so affected by the music that my eyes welled with tears to the point that I had to pull my car to the side of the road. I prayed in a way that I remember to this day. I said, "Jesus, I will follow you even if it means I will not have another friend in my life." I often wonder if my motivation for living in Christian community grew out of a desire to assure others who may be praying similar prayers that they will not have to go through this alone.

There's very little that happens at Solomon's Porch without being seriously thought through. Even the pieces of our community life that are spontaneous and improvisational are outgrowths of deep consideration of who we are and the people we are seeking to become. This applies to everything from the time we meet to the art on the walls.

with some deciding instead to sculpt Christian monsters, black widow spiders, and other violent things. I tried to encourage them to stick to their parables. I feel grateful that these children, some of whom have parents who have passed away or are imprisoned, are here in our community, where they can be encouraged and nurtured. ·

2/2/03

The worship gathering on Sunday was very unusual because Doug was gone. It consisted of communion, lots of reading, and tons of music by various artists in the community. It was great to hear so many different people's expressions, but I definitely missed having a message. I was the greeter for the gathering, which is a fun job for me. I love welcoming new people and hearing their stories about why and from where they came to Solomon's Porch.

DUSTIN

Now, kids at the church are a whole different deal. I don't have kids. I'm not around kids. And I'm not anti-kid, unless by anti-kid you mean I don't like them. I have such a difficult time focusing on the sermon anyway, even without kids running around distracting me. The elementary kids are off in the corner chatting it up, the toddlers are running around beating anything in sight with a wooden mallet, and the crying kids are just put in the back of the room.

Somehow, by moving a screaming kid 10 feet, parents think that it doesn't bother anyone.

No matter where you sit, you are destined to be near children. I'm trying to not be

Because our gatherings are designed to be interactive and participatory, our furniture is set in the round so we can see one another. This helps us engage one another during the music, prayer, and discussion times. Admittedly, this has been a stretch for us Minnesotans who don't like to draw attention to ourselves. But over time, we've gotten used to seeing faces in church rather than the backs of heads.

We have also chosen to not use the concert metaphor for our worship. Since the 1880s one of the dominant metaphors for church structures has been the theatre. In the 1960s, this evolved to the concert setting, which hung onto the stage-focused environment with performers on one level and the audience on another. The use of stages, lighting, and electric sound reinforcement of music and voice has become so commonplace in most churches that most of us never question why it's there. While this format is familiar and works well for the communication of a single message to large settings of people, it also has a limiting effect on the ability of the body to engage collectively in communal worship. Attention is directed toward the stage and the words coming from it. The relationship is between me as an audience member and the speaker, not me and my fellow audience members.

We had a few choices of the kind of seating we could pursue for our worship gathering, the pew, the "theater" seat, and the couch. They each bring with them the expectation of a different outcome. The theater seat invokes a feeling of wanting to be entertained. The pew brings anticipation of a lecture. The couch brings about notions of home. You can probably guess why we chose the couch.

Part of our communal effort on Sunday nights is to limit the things that separate those in charge from those who are not; our hope is that all people will be part of this experience. That's why it's important that the roles people play not be confused with power in other areas of our community. We don't have special places of activity or certain rights that are reserved for only some (okay, I admit we do have gender-specific rest rooms). Because we don't have a stage, we don't have to be concerned with who is utilizing that place of power. It is important for us not to centralize power or give undue power to those wearing microphones who speak to the entire group in ways that others do not have. We are conscious of the feelings that come when one person has the ability to address the crowd with sophisticated sound reinforcement and what that communicates to others about whose words are important.

Because of the couches, the absence of a stage, and the fact that people wander around during the gathering, some people describe our setting as casual. Actually, I prefer the word *normal*. But what happens in this space is anything but normal.

When we gather in our normal-looking living room-like space, it is so we can talk about the unusual things of God and the call to live a life in the Kingdom of God. We infuse abnormal practices into this normal place. We sing, pray, confess, profess, eat the body and drink the blood of our Savior, sit quietly, hear the story of God, hear each other's stories, and give money because these are practices that we want to replicate in the rest of our lives. If we can only talk about these things in highly regulated places, then we will have a difficult time translating what is talked about here to any other setting. We are seeking to create a place where our normal lives intersect with the intentional structuring of life in the Christian practices. In this we hope to learn how to bring the two together in other settings. Instead of having a special place, unlike any other, where we try to make the things of God seem normal, we have tried to create a normal place that gives us permission to discuss the unique things of God.

Our current church space and our previous one are both in areas of Minneapolis with a high concentration of alternative cultures. Our previous neighborhood was the center for well-educated, sophisticated cultural creatives who shop at the natural foods co-op and drive Volvos.

Our current neighborhood space is much the same: in a poor neighborhood with a higher concentration of the aggressive anti-World Trade Organization types and those representing the "limit urban sprawl" movements. Both of these settings have provided us with wonderful opportunities to live in the way of Jesus, not just because of all the outreach we can do, but because we have so much to learn from them. In addition to their input on serious cultural issues, we have the chance to live into our peculiarities of faith.

When I tell people from other areas of Minneapolis where our church is, they often mention the weird, vaguely New Age notions prevalent in these neighborhoods. While I'm not interested in defending any funky New Age beliefs, I'm often struck that so many Christians think that what they do and believe is so normal. To me, the compelling part of the Kingdom call is its unusual nature, not that it is some run-of-the-mill, everyday belief. I'm not sure exactly what people are referring to when they talk about "the strange beliefs" of alternative cultures, but it's got to be really out there if it's going to out-strange a faith that professes a Savior of the world who was born of a virgin, walked on water,

agitated by them and appreciate them for whatever I'm supposed to appreciate them for, but for someone who hasn't been exposed to children it can be tough.

Church without Doug is a lot like when Valerie left on that old sitcom Valerie's Family. Once Shelly Duncan took off, the show became The Hogan Family and went straight downhill. Doug is our Valerie. Each week he is gone brings us one step closer to syndication.

Actually, this week was very good. Our bandleader's cousin performed a 40 minute theater piece where he acted out something like 40 characters from the Bible. All of the people he moved in and out of were characters Jesus interacted with in one way or another. The leper, Zechariah, Peter, Judas, Lazarus. It was fascinating to think about these simple encounters from a totally new perspective. Instead of the usual "read aloud" method, the acting out allowed us to see things not from a narrator's point of view but from the person Jesus touched. How would the leper have reacted to Jesus' blessing after a lifetime of sickness? What would Judas's last few hours been like, internally wrestling with the notion of selling out the Son of God?

————

Somehow Kristin and I usually end up talking about religion or the Porch. It could be our similar backgrounds, our interest in the topics, or that we just have zero history together. We talked about

healed people with his spit, died a death that had meaning enough to defeat sin and death in all the universe, rose from the dead, and promised a physical return and a remade heaven and earth. We are the people of peculiar beliefs and practices. It is these particular practices that help form us on Sunday nights.

GATHERING PIECES

Since the beginning of Solomon's Porch, we have done things in particular, and often peculiar, ways. But we have worked very hard not to be peculiar for the sake of novelty. We are more interested in creating authentic practices than interesting or trendy practices. When making decisions about what we will do we regularly ask the questions, "Does this fit us?" and "Are we acting in a natural way?" more often than "Is this something that will attract new people?" Authenticity is more valuable to us than slick production or professional execution. We would prefer to have people speak, sing, and create with sincerity than with polish. We are haunted by the image of the falsely friendly sales clerk who calls strangers "honey" and acts like your best friend even as he swipes your credit card. We'd rather he just act like us, and hope people are warmly greeted.

Our Sunday gatherings combine regular elements with occasional surprises. While special inclusions are always welcome and add variety, it is in the routine practices that we find our rhythm for living.

MUSIC

The music we use in our gatherings is a homegrown expression of our faith. We have a disproportionate number of talented musicians who write and perform our music. We have a repertoire of songs that we rotate through, so we're able to bring both freshness and familiarity to our singing. In our community the role of music extends beyond mere praise and worship. Our songs serve to instruct, to teach, to call, to plead, and to express; music is narrative, it's prayer, it's a physical discipline. Some songs are meant to be sung by all and others wash over us. Because our music is written by us, it is both personal and communal. When our community joins together with those who have created the music, the words and melody come alive and dwell among us. There is so much of Christian expression that is ethereal and conceptual, but singing songs written by our friends grounds our worship in the here and now. Corey knows the lives of his friends here, so when he writes a song that pleads for God to create something new in us, he is giving voice to the longings of our community.

Songs are not just words we sing—they are invitations into a way of life. Writing our own songs allows us to have an expression of faith that is true to us and our world. They give us a place to say, "This is what we believe. This is what we confess. These are not the words of others; they are in agreement with others, but they are our songs."

Some find it strange that we use historical pieces for our invocation, confessions, and prayers and then write our own music. I understand what they're getting at, but we believe we are called to confess the faith of the ages and the faith of today. We have decided to use music for today and the other elements for the ages.

We have also chosen to create our own sermons. This is not a necessary practice; there have been more than enough wonderful sermons preached in this world that we could go a long time without creating anything new. But in our community there is a high value placed on having homegrown sermons. And so it goes with our music.

Our music is certainly one of our most distinctive elements, so it garners a great deal of conversation and curiosity. I've found that people often assume we use our own music because we have something against the music of other churches or other generations. Anyone who tries to take us down that road doesn't understand in the least bit what we are doing. We use our own music precisely because we honor the music of our predecessors. Our desire is to make our contribution to the beautiful legacy of music in the church.

One of the roles of the church through the centuries has been to put faith into stories and songs that fit their day. This is what we're doing. Because we're committed to being a community that not only benefits from the Church that has gone before it, but contributes to the Church that will follow us, we want to do all we can to implore our in-house poets and musicians to create.

For us music is not understood as preparation for learning, it *is* learning. It is not a precursor to worship, it *is* worship. It is more than a cognitive slide show of hopeful escapism. It's one way that we physically express our faith. For us worship is not fanatisizing about somewhere else but an attempt to create a place of physical participation in the life of God with our bodies, in a place, with a certain group of people and a very real God.

church the first time we hung out. That's never happened before, and yet it's somewhat empowering to have someone that you don't know that well, or more importantly doesn't know you that well, to talk about this sort of thing with. I don't know why that is, but I've always had a tough time discussing faith with people I had established relationships with: High school friends, college buddies, parents. We were never that good at talking about God. Maybe it's because I had an "image" to uphold or something. Some unconscious side of me felt that by discussing God it made me weaker or something. I don't know. I just know I appreciate Kristin for this new conversation outlet.

Tonight we talked about the Porch's style for

dealing with beginner Christians. I was raised in the belief that you had a certain set of words you had to say in order for Jesus to "come in" and wrap things up. The Porch doesn't do this, and for a while it bothered me.

They do, however, regularly run through Bible 101. "For those of you that don't know, the Bible is divided into two parts, the Old Testament and the New Testament. There are 66 books in the Bible, and the first four in the New Testament are called the Gospels written by . . ." I started to realize that was the Porch's way of getting new Christians comfortable with the Bible.

It's how the Porch welcomes people of any background and knowledge base to feel more comfortable. It keeps the Porch

PSALM

Each Sunday night has a rhythm of its own, but we nearly always begin with our same liturgy–a song and a psalm and another song. Normally we read the psalm in its entirety (other than Psalm 119, which is frankly far too long for our structure, so we read it according to it's books). There is no explanation of the psalm, it is simply read. In some ways this is an interaction with the poetry of our faith. As with many of our interactions with the Bible we are careful to not overlay too much of our interpretation or explanation on the text. The experience of having the psalm wash over us is plenty powerful; it doesn't really need our help.

We always have women read the psalm and most other Bible passages we use. Unfortunately most people have heard the Bible read in a man's voice far more often than a woman's voice. The voices of women speaking the words inspired by God creates a beautiful moment of worship.

The woman reading the psalm does something else that strikes people as odd on their first visit to our gatherings. The reader simply stands up where she is and reads—sometimes from the projected words on the big screens, sometimes from a Bible in her hand. There is almost an element of surprise for the people sitting next to the psalm reader. There they are minding their own business, taking the whole thing in, and suddenly the person next to or behind them stands and reads, as if she's in charge. And for that moment, she is. There is a change in people's experience that comes from where the content of the worship gathering originates. When the person leading is next to or behind you, it has a way of drawing you in and making you part of the experience.

STORY

From this point, the order of elements will shift from week to week, but all the pieces will be there. One of the elements I look forward to each week is the story. We all come with one, participate in each other's, and are part of God's, so it makes sense to incorporate these stories into our community life. We invite people to share their stories, to listen to someone else's, and to allow the story of God to provide a better understanding of both.

I need to point out that sharing our stories is not the same thing as giving our testimonies. At times that's what happens, but just as often people share poetry or music they've written or talk about a ministry they're involved in or are moving into. There are times when the story is explicitly about things of faith and times when it is about struggles or successes. There is no agenda for these stories—even I don't always know what a person is going to say when they agree to share their story at a gathering. While not sounding like "testimonies" in the traditional sense, these stories of the ways God bubbles up in others' lives serve as testaments to who God is and how God acts in our lives. Telling and hearing these stories shapes us and forms us.

HISTORICAL PIECE

There is also great value in the stories of the past. Each week we read a creed, prayer, or collect. This is a significant element for many of us, especially those of us from Protestant backgrounds for whom 500 years ago is ancient history. Saying the words of those who lived and worshiped in the second century places our faith in the context of something bigger than our time and our concerns. We receive a broader vision of who God is and has always been. It allows us to see ourselves as a small part of something big rather than a big part of something small.

COMMUNION

We participate in communion every week at Solomon's Porch. For us, the practice of communion has gone beyond a ritual and moved into the realm of necessity. There are people in our community for whom communion is a kind of litmus test for how comfortable they will be in a church. Some come from backgrounds where communion is so steeped in ritual that, for them, it's lost its meaning. Others come from traditions where communion was an infrequent event or one that was seen primarily as a remembrance of an old Bible story.

The experiences of all of these people have moved us to take great pains to make communion a time where we are not just looking back on an event, but also looking inward and looking forward.

Many weeks we ask people to consider Jesus' statement to his disciples on the night of the Last Supper: "And he said to them, 'I have eagerly desired to eat this Passover with you before I suffer. For I tell you, I will not eat it again until it finds fulfillment in the Kingdom of God'" (Luke 22:15–16). For Jesus the meaning of the new understanding of the Passover meal was not limited to the past, it was found in the present and future. So we attempt to look forward to the day when the Kingdom of God plays out the way it was meant to be.

Jesus used many metaphors to help people understand the Kingdom of God, including comparing it to a king who wanted to have a huge party. We have framed our communion time around that notion of a respectful house party in which we talk and embrace and offer the bread and the cup to one another.

from having a high turnover of "summer camp converts" and really works on gaining a rhythm in everyday life.

—

Church was new and different. In order to not only talk about but also actually do things differently for the special Easter service, the couches were arranged in small-group formations that allowed us to stare at each other and talk about the Easter Story. It reminded me of AA and affirmation time, but whatever, we all shared. It was a bit odd sitting there with several good friends and my folks going, "Here's what God is doing in my life." Nothing too hot to cover, just that isn't an area my folks and I take up too often. That is what I appreciate about the church. It's helped me open up about my faith.

Instead of changing the subject and talking about monkeys or something, I've gotten to the point where I can hold a faith conversation, in front of real people, for more than two minutes. The Porch's openness and hospitality to everyone has acted as a catalyst to communication for friends and family alike. All because we encourage interaction and getting involved in every aspect of each other's lives. Well, that and the free food.

JIM
3/23

Tonight at church I wept. We were blessed with a group of Guatemalans who came to SP to pray for our group that will soon visit the country to build houses. I cried because the prayers were so fervent and beautiful. They were spoken in Spanish,

When we experience communion in a social interaction, we are not being social, we are trying to remember this meal signifies both the sacrifice of the past and the promise that someday the Kingdom of God will be here, and we will eat this meal again in its fullness.

To create this situation we set elements around the room, and people serve one another. It is not special people who give these ordinary elements meaning. It is we as ordinary people serving one another special elements. The bread is good quality and full of taste. Both juice and wine are available in a common cup or individual cups.

We begin communion with an introduction from someone in our community. This person offers his or her perspective on the significance of communion, and it's incredible to hear the range of experiences and understandings. While they frame the introduction the way they want, we do ask them to include this saying that we created to give a consistency to the way we think about communion in our community:

"We take communion by serving and eating bread and wine together, in community with followers of Jesus around the world and throughout all ages. We enter this mystery proclaiming and having faith in Jesus as the Messiah, whose life, death, burial, resurrection, and ascension show the love of God for the world, free us from sin, and initiate the Kingdom of God in our world in new ways, for the benefit and blessing of all creation."

With these words in our heads and hearts, we take and eat.

PRAYER

We have found that most people who come to our gatherings really do want to live in harmony with God and want to pray regardless of how religious they may be. Most people who are not familiar with the things of Christianity who visit us on Sunday nights are more interested in participating in the Christian things we do than in simply hearing about them. Yet many of us struggle with prayer because our means of prayer are so limited. On Sunday nights we seek to not only have significant times of prayer, but also to model various forms of prayer. We believe that God is a personal God who listens to and answers our prayers. Our prayer times include verbal and nonverbal expressions. Sometimes we offer prayers out loud; other times we are silent or use physical postures to convey the mood or striving of our prayers. We might use our own words or read an ancient or historical prayer as a way of connecting with the passions of those who have gone before us. Our prayer room is open during the gathering so that anyone who wants to pray in solitude or continue their prayers after we've moved on to other things has a place to do so.

SERMON

Most weeks we look at part of the Bible during a time that we refer to as the sermon. I tend to be careful about using that word, not because I'm afraid to have my words be known as a sermon, but because they may not rise to the level of what others require a sermon to be. This time is centered on a chapter or two from the book of the Bible in which we are spending time. The sermon basically consists of me reading these parts with a running commentary that we refer to as a sermon. This commentary includes historical clarification as well as reflections on what may be of consequence for our community. This commentary is a group effort, having been shaped the previous Tuesday in our Bible discussion group where we preview the reading for the coming Sunday and talk through its implications as we work to enter into what it has to say.

The Bible is our primary text for the sermon. I don't typically quote other people. I don't lay out a three-point thesis or make a great effort to apply what we're reading to life today. Instead, we want to know the story of God and see our lives in relationship to what God is doing, has done, and promises to do.

The story of God is the story that encompasses our entire life. Our hope for the sermon is that it allows us to find ourselves in that story, to see how others have played their part, and be informed by the ways they followed God. Reading the Bible through this lens offers a tremendous perspective for those of us who tend to get stuck in the muck of today.

On most occasions the sermon is followed by a time of open discussion where I ask for comments, interpretations, and thoughts of significance from our community. During these few minutes not only are brilliant observations made, but people are also reminded that we are called to listen to one another and be taught by each other and not only by the pastor.

CHILDREN

We love children at Solomon's Porch and very much desire for them to be part of our community. Our intention on Sunday nights is to create an atmosphere that is conducive for children's spiritual formation. Our children are part of the worship gathering all the way through.

and I was moved by the realization that God's Kingdom includes people from every race, tongue, and culture. God cannot be contained by our "Western mind-set." I felt a closeness and friendship to these visitors, like they were my family, because of this common bond of Christ.

2/2/03

Tonight Carla is hosting the church meeting since Doug is out of town. She asked me to introduce the Apostles' Creed. This must be some sort of providence, if I dare say so. I've been reading Clapp and Webber's, A People of the Truth, and in it they discuss how our worldview must be so shaped by the story of Jesus that it leads us to BE a certain kind of people with peculiar practices and a peculiar character. The Apostles'

Creed reminds me of this. It has stated for more than 1,800 years what we Christians are to believe. But the implicit understanding of the Creed is that anyone who believes such things should live in a peculiar kind of way. We are to be people who freely give, forgive, live without fear of death, live as though we are not our own masters, and who live with and for each other. Could there be any other way to live as someone who confesses God to be creator, redeemer, the one who resurrects the dead, the forgiver of sins, the creator of a community of saints who will reign forever? Having the opportunity to introduce this creed will definitely be an important moment for me. I feel as if God is calling me to be more vocal, and doing this is a good first step.

When we started Solomon's Porch, the only children joining us were mine. But over the last three years, we've seen the number of children explode. We're not just adding babies, but elementary-aged children as well. Let me introduce you to Colleen Shealer. She is part of our paid staff and coordinates our efforts to involve children in our worship gatherings.

While it is my job to invite people into our work with children, I am not the only one who takes the spiritual formation of our children seriously. It really is a community effort. Because the order of happenings on Sunday nights changes from week to week the point at which the toddlers and preschoolers meet in their "pink and orange room" changes. On this night it is early in the evening during the Invocation when I hand off baby Duke to Carla, so I can unlock the door. As I open the door a handful of toddlers and preschoolers run toward the room to join Angelie and Chris, tonight's "room hosts." The hosts coordinate a fifteen minute time of engagement with the toddlers that includes free-play, a snack, a game, and on occasion, as much as I hate to admit it, a short video. But for most of the toddlers the highlight of the evening comes over the next 20 minutes during their "spiritual formation experience" down in the kitchen. We are working toward forming practices that allow our toddlers and preschoolers to enter into communal life with God on Sunday evenings. Tonight, Laura and Matt shuffle the group downstairs where this week's experience will include the creation and singing of music. The other weekly "experiences" include art, dance, story, and sensory activities. These five practices allow spiritual formation to occur within meaningful, age-appropriate physical expressions. This range of experiences is made possible with the involvement of our musicians, artists, dancers, and storytellers. We want our children to know this is a safe place to dance, sing, create, and tell their stories, and a place where they are encouraged to the fullness of God.

Tonight I witness something beautiful going on in our kitchen: Laura leading singing, Matt playing with a toddler, and two-year-olds learning how to be a part of the Kingdom of God in our community.

Back upstairs as we begin the sermon time, the elementary-aged kids meet me in their blue room along the back of our gathering space. They spend the first few minutes messing around and then start begging me to tell them what we're working on tonight—it is good to see their enthusiasm. I explain that the elementary-aged children will be providing one of the installations for our Good Friday "Way of the Cross" event. We're "doing" Peter denies Christ. I ask them to share times when they felt betrayed.

Chachrista tells us about the time her classmate told everyone her secret. Connor reflects on the story told earlier in the worship gathering by Anette about how she was ridiculed and excluded when she was a child because of her skin color. (I can't help but smile when I consider that these children really do understand adult conversations and are being formed when they are part of the worship gathering.) As it turns out each child has a story of betrayal. I ask them to create a piece of artwork depicting their experience. We head out of the room and parade to the tables set up in the main gathering space where we spend the next 15 to 20 minutes listening to the sermon, sharing and "stealing" markers, intently drawing, and bravely exposing secrets of betrayal. What a great way to be part of a worship gathering: listening, sharing, and creating.

About the time the sermon ends and the elementary kids disperse back to their parents, the group of toddlers and preschoolers silently stomp up the stairs. The kids slowly work their way through the maze of couches, stopping to talk to that guy with the funny hair, or to nibble on some leftover communion bread. As the children find their place it becomes clear that spiritual formation in our community is not only for adults. In some ways it is the children who lead us.

One of the significant concerns we had in our early days of the effort was that our children would be left in the dust as we blazed a new trail for our own spirituality. I remember on more than one occasion wondering if our four children would hit their adult years and say, "Mom and Dad, you know when we were doing that hippy-wannabe church thing? I didn't learn anything, and I wish I had." I can happily say that three years into this our children and the others of Solomon's Porch are experiencing an integrated physical faith. It's an expression of faith that is not attempting to lead them to a better cognitive understanding, but one that finds validity in its own right. It's our way of recognizing that they are no more required to have faith figured out than we are and that their process of becoming Christian will take a lifetime, not an hour. Our children may not know all the superstars of flannelgraph faith, but they are learning the ways of physical faith, prayer, and confession.

JAVIER

The weirdest thing last night was not the music or the poetry (actually some Bible passages that were poetic), which was for the most part all right. The weird part of the night was that someone brought these Styrofoam cups that said "I (Heart Symbol) America." I am not sure where they were from because we have people bring food each week. It was really strange that we had them. I was talking to Brett (our current drummer–a really good player) about it, and we were reflecting on the role of government in the spiritual life of the people of God. It was a brief conversation during one of the other songs that evening, but we both agreed that we like the separation of church and state, and that maybe Christians would be better off if it were left intact.

3.6.2003

The Ash Wednesday gathering at SP last night was good. It began with people walking a labyrinth, which is always an enjoyable yet scary thing for me to do. If you have never done it, drop this book and go find a place where you can experience it for the first time. It really is an experience that takes you out of yourself and carries you into the holy.

As I was walking it last night I felt like maybe the OT priests did when they went into the holy of holies. There was excitement and fear. I felt like I should have taken my shoes off to walk it. You know, that holy ground thing...

After the labyrinth, we went upstairs to the gathering space and prayed and sang and had the ashes placed on

ART

Art is a regular part of our worship experience and ranges from performance art to visual art. We use projection screens to guide our songs, prayers, and collective readings, but we don't just slap the words up on the screen. Michelle puts significant effort into creating images that work with the words to lead us to new places. There are times when the image is more transformative than the words.

Art is also hung on our walls. One of the long walls of our meeting space is actually a row of offices. Each of these offices has a window or wood panel, 14 in all, that we use to display artwork correlating to the church season. As I'm writing this, we have entered the season of Pentecost, and Luke created charcoal sketches depicting the apostles at the time of Pentecost. We lit a tea light candle above each apostle's head on the day of Pentecost. These panels were used to display the stations of the cross during Easter, and are the home of in-house works of art during other seasons of the year. Our art serves as a subtle, yet moving way of drawing us into our story of our faith.

GIVING

Giving is a sore spot in many churches. Some pastors worry that talking too much about giving is a turnoff for young Christians, and in some ways, they are right. When tithes are presented as one more financial commitment required of already debt-ridden 20- and 30-somethings, there is bound to be a struggle. At Solomon's Porch we have tried to frame our understanding of giving by thinking of tithing as part of the process of spiritual formation. We see tithing as something we do, not only to support the work of the church, but also as a way of organizing even the financial parts of our lives around life with God. We can talk about money in this way because we talk about everything else in this way.

But because the financial part of our life as a community is really just one more practice of our faith, we are able to talk very openly about what our needs are and what we should do to meet those needs. Our giving of money is connected to our community's contributions in other ways. We have recently added a time when we recognize contributions of service to our community or to the poor. We acknowledge contributions of cleaning our space or adding artwork. We use this time as a reminder that we are all called not only to receive but also to give. We are called not to consume, but to participate and bless. We remind one another of our place in financially participating in our community. There is no formal time of collecting contributions, so each is able to put their money in one of the receptacles when they are prepared to do so.

BLESSING

We end our gatherings with a sung blessing. We do this with the recognition that life is bigger than all of us, that we all need a blessing as we venture out into the rest of our lives. We need others around us who can speak the truth of God to us and give us God's encouragement. We stand together and sing. Some hold hands, some wrap arms around others, some bounce a child or dance with a toddler as we send one another out to do the work we've been given to do.

...

Having tried to describe our Sunday night worship gathering, I am caught by two feelings. On one hand perhaps I have made things to sound better than they are or created the impression that this comes easily and we are confident in ourselves. Believe me, our efforts are not as neat and tidy as they may sound. But they are sincere efforts, and through them we are being formed by practices that we could not maintain outside of a community.

At the same time I have the sense that I have not nearly done our evenings justice. I simply do not have the skill to put into words what happens in us and through us during our gatherings. There is more going on than I have described or could ever completely reveal.

I wish that we could spend time in each other's worlds and worship in each other's places. Maybe then we would have eyes to see and ears to hear what God has been saying to one another's churches.

Until then I would like to leave you with one of the blessings we sing each Sunday night to each other and for each other.

our foreheads. I wouldn't change a thing except the songs. I think they were good songs, but Ben's voice was too pretty in those songs to really convey repentance and brokenness. No big deal...just an observation.

After the Easter breakfast Sarah and I came home and took a nap. It was good to take a nap because I hardly ever take them. Then we went to the gathering on Sunday night.

It was a good gathering, although it was a little different in its style as there was no sermon time, and it was more dialogue oriented as we sat around in groups and read pieces of the resurrection story and ate smoked fish and crackers.

The music was good, though. I played a new song tonight in my fur-

ther attempts at putting the whole mass to music and also helping to bring liturgy to the life of SP. It is a simple melody, as I think that liturgy should be some-thing that all peo-ple should be able to sing after listen-ing to it a couple of times.

The song is "Agnus Dei." Here is the lyric:

Agnus Dei
O Christ, Lamb of God
That takes away
the sin of the
world
Have mercy on us
Have mercy on us
O Christ, Lamb of God
That takes away
the sin of the
world
Grant us your
peace
Grant us your
peace
O Christ, Lamb of God
That takes away
the sin of the
world
Have mercy on us
Have mercy on us

Go in Peace

Go in peace;
Seeking on;
United bought and freed.

In times of trial
Our hopes should be
Spirit filled
And holy.

May you be
Eternally
Blessed and wonderfully

Led all your days
By love's pure light
Prayerful in
All ways.

Sow in peace;
Dream of a place;
Love in the name of the Lord.
Amen.

Go in peace
May Christ surround you.
The Kingdom of God has no end.
Amen. Amen. Amen. Amen. 2x

CHAPTER 04

SPIRITUAL FORMATION THROUGH PHYSICALITY

MONDAY

It's 6:15 on Monday night. People will start arriving at my home for our weekly yoga class. My name is Katherine Kleingartner. I've been leading these classes since we started them a year ago.

Tonight, as I do every Monday, I have a series of poses prepared, like a lesson plan, in advance. But typically, my plans change once the class begins because someone may have a particular need, or the group as a whole is exhibiting fatigue—or, conversely, a lot of extra energy. We aren't here for a hardcore physical workout as much as the chance to be together, to breathe, to relax, and to bring ourselves to a place of peace and gratitude. My lesson plan is intended to facilitate that process, not dictate it.

As we begin, everyone sits on colorful blue, purple, green, and orange yoga mats, ready to stretch our arms and lower backs. This is a warming-up period, a time to settle in and move beyond our chattiness. It is how we begin to let go of the troubles from our days. Soon, conversation is replaced with sighs and groans as we regulate our breathing and become aware of our stiff joints and aching muscles.

Then we move on to our poses. These vary from week to week, but Downward Facing Dog is a must. The body of a person in Downward Dog looks like an inverted V—palms flat on the floor, hips high in the air, balls of the feet anchoring the other side of the V. When done correctly, this posture stretches almost every muscle of the body and reveals the personality of an individual's joints and muscles. It shows me the flexibility of a student's hamstrings, shoulders, and back and the strength each person possesses. As the instructor I can use this information in future postures to make certain no one is injured.

We flow from one pose to another like a dance, concentrating on our bodies and our breathing as we move.

ERIN

1/27/03

I went to yoga class on Monday evening. It was packed with people, some from church and some of Katherine's friends. Yoga has been a great outlet for me for years, so I was delighted to find it as a communal activity at Solomon's Porch. To be physical with a group of people is an amazing way to build connections and trust. On a personal level, I love yoga because I tend to internalize stress, so to spend an hour focusing on the breath and releasing tension from my muscles is a wonderful way to increase wellness.

3 March, 2003

I went to Katherine's yoga class right after my lessons. For the first time in weeks, I really struggled with yoga. My body was tight and sore, but throughout the class my

Sometimes we hold a pose so long and focus so hard that I must remind students to breathe. Breath that flows in and out is essential for a body to move and flex. A body in which breath is held looks rigid, as if it's trying to hold on to everything. But a body in which breath flows has a face of contentment and easiness. I'm often struck by how difficult it is to remember to breathe. It is our most unconscious action, and yet we can forget how to do it well when our minds are busy with other things.

We balance, we fold, we exert, we rest. After 45 minutes the concentration in the room is palpable. Chit-chat has completely stopped, and even my jokes go unacknowledged. This tells me that tension has been released from the muscles, inner chatter has moved out of the brain, and self-awareness and peacefulness have settled in. My voice becomes quieter as I talk us through one pose and into the next. From my vantage point in front of the class, I see students synchronized, standing with arms stretched forward and legs folded or pointed. They look like herons about to take flight. It is beautiful to see people quiet and poised and balanced. Faces relax, breath comes easily. We are simultaneously disciplined and passive, both strong and accepting.

Our last pose of the evening is called "savasana" (pronounced sha-va-sa-na) or corpse pose. The student lies on her back letting the legs fall open as they will, the arms hang limp like empty coat sleeves. The face, the forehead, the space between the eyebrows all relax, and the person melts heavily into the floor. Eyes are closed, breathing is rhythmic. I turn the lights off, and only the glow of candles and sometimes the fireplace illuminates the room.

This state of being is holy. It is at this time that we become closer to God, aware of our bodies, of the divine. The clutter that competes with God's presence in our lives has fallen away, and we are open to God's love and God's will. We are soft and vulnerable, knowing that we get stuck, and we thank God for this opportunity to get unstuck.

It is with this gratitude that we end the evening. On my instruction, students ever so slowly bring themselves up to a seated position, heads bowed. We lift our hands to our hearts in a prayer position and silently think of three things we are grateful for. Then I ask each person to send prayer out to someone who is in need, and we open our hands as if presenting all that we have. On nights when the group is small and more intimate, we might hold hands as we pray in silence.

I thank everyone for coming. People are free to stand and leave, but most remain quiet for a little while. I stand to switch on a lamp. Slowly people get up, talk, commit to a daily practice of yoga in hopes of getting this feeling again and again. We are hesitant to leave this moment of shared reverence, this experience of worship.

...

When people discover that we're a church with a yoga class, that a massage therapist uses part of our space, and that we are home to many who choose a simple organic lifestyle, they sometimes assume that we're simply out to appeal to the cultural creatives and neo-hippies.

In fact, what these things represent is our desire as a community to live whole Kingdom lives, lives in which the very act of being provides connectedness to God and is a blessing to others. We are seeking to be formed into people living in harmony with God through what we do with our bodies as well as what we do with our hearts, souls, and minds.

For the call to Kingdom life was never limited to just one part of ourselves. Even those who would agree that the body is the "temple of the Holy Spirit" and therefore worth caring for can be wary of physical expressions such as yoga or alternative medicine because of the dust of the New Age movement that settles around these ways of living. The idea that how we move, how we eat, how we heal might affect our faith is consistent with the long Christian history we are seeking to live into. This is not something started with a particular need of the church to reach out to any particular people but is inherent in our faith dating to its earliest times.

In the Old Testament the people of God were called to lives of physical rest and worship, of dietary restrictions, of mandated fabric in their wardrobes. They understood that certain ceremonial worship practices could open them up to God in new ways. They believed that the rhythms and needs of the body were not only designed by God, but also were a means toward experiencing God.

When New Testament Christians wanted to be "saved," Peter instructed them to join the community of faith by doing physical things—undergoing baptism, selling their belongings, meeting daily, serving, preaching, feeding.

Acts 15 quotes a letter sent from the church leaders in Jerusalem to those coming to faith in Jesus who were not of Jewish background. It reads,

muscles became less resistant and let me move flexibly. I still finished class with the balanced and relaxed feeling with which I usually end the class. Afterward, Shana and I stayed a while and talked with Katherine and James about natural healing and intuition. We are all amazed at the number of healers at Solomon's Porch and feel grateful for the graces they bring to our lives. I spent the rest of my evening studying physics and reading the Bible.

4 March, 2003
Fat Tuesday. I have decided to give up sweets for Lent. My Catholic roots have instilled in me that it is important to deny myself something during this liturgical season in order to try to better understand the sufferings of Christ. Sweets are the only thing to which I am addicted, so they seem to be

the best thing to abstain from. I have unsuccessfully tried to stop eating sweets twice this year. Both times I quickly gave up after experiencing periods of shakiness and lightheadedness. This time I am prepared to suffer and determined to have control over my body. Tonight, though, I said goodbye that was more sweet than bittersweet and polished off nearly a pint of ice cream while I studied.

5 March 2003
After work and a few classes, I ran home where my friend Jill was waiting for me. The two of us went to church for the Ash Wednesday gathering. Jill has high energy and is hilarious, and the two of us entered church giggly and lighthearted, which was horribly poorly timed for an event that is designed to be introspective and somber. After

With them they sent the following letter:

The apostles and elders, your brothers,

To the Gentile believers in Antioch, Syria and Cilicia:

Greetings.

We have heard that some went out from us without our authorization and disturbed you, troubling your minds by what they said. So we all agreed to choose some men and send them to you with our dear friends Barnabas and Paul—men who have risked their lives for the name of our Lord Jesus Christ. Therefore we are sending Judas and Silas to confirm by word of mouth what we are writing. It seemed good to the Holy Spirit and to us not to burden you with anything beyond the following requirements: You are to abstain from food sacrificed to idols, from blood, from the meat of strangled animals and from sexual immorality. You will do well to avoid these things.

Farewell. (Acts 15:23-29)

The letter emphasizes the importance of keeping a faith that is lived in the body, while at the same time moving beyond the mandate of the "Old Testament Covenant." These new converts to the way of Jesus did not have the cultural or religious history of the nation of Israel, yet all the encouragements to their faith focused on belief as it plays out in physical life.

Similarly, Jesus lived an integrated, whole Kingdom life of physical spirituality. Jesus shared meals with his friends. He walked the dirt roads with them. He healed them with the touch of his hands. He used his spit to restore sight to a blind man. He washed the grime from the feet of his disciples. These moments of physicality are not incidental to our understanding of who Jesus was and is—they give us permission to trust that God really is present in the mundane, physical acts of our own lives.

God and the physical world interacting in harmony—this is the story of Jesus. We see it in the birth of the savior through the body of a young virgin. We see it in the crucifixion of Jesus, which served as the coming together of the things of God and the things of the body for the reconciliation of all creation. We certainly see it in Jesus' physical resurrection, the great proof of the validity of his ministry. What Jesus did was not otherworldly, it was perfectly worldly.

We are invited into that same life. Just as Jesus lived faith in his body, so we as followers of Jesus are invited to be his body on earth with our bodies. This is not to deny the mind nor to denigrate the intellect. Instead it is in recognition that we are whole people called and able to live complete, integrated lives. And so we at Solomon's Porch use physicality as a means of spiritual formation.

JIM
3/5/03

Tonight was Ash Wednesday and a real blessing. I've desperately wanted to keep exploring "high liturgy," because it has offered me the chance to be molded and shaped in ways that Christians have been molded for 2,000 years. Though SP is not a high liturgical church, the service we participated in seems so consistent with the ethos of this church. God can and does speak to us through many ways, including symbols, smells, sounds, and our sight. For me, the physical touch of the ashes on my face and the act of being marked with the cross of Christ, "forgiven in grace," was so powerful. To then be one who assisted Doug in marking others with ashes was even more powerful, especially when the children came forward. As a father of two, it is such an incredible thing to say to a child that God will "bring us all to the joy of your resurrection." It is such an incredibly humbling experience to mark someone, to stand between a person and their act of worship of God; to see Frank breathe deeply and almost fall backward as he was marked. This was not only worship for them, but also worship for me.

THE INTERSECTION OF BODY AND SPIRIT

About seven years ago my wife was diagnosed with endometriosis, a very serious disease of the reproductive organs. Shelley followed the advice of her gynecologist and underwent multiple surgeries, including a complete hysterectomy, but the disease returned. She was one of the statistical anomalies of an otherwise successful medical regime. (The truth of the matter is that it doesn't matter what percentage of people are helped by the procedure if it doesn't work for you—for Shelley, it was a 100 percent failure.) Not knowing what to do next, and feeling a lack of confidence in the traditional approach we'd been using, she started to consider some natural health alternatives. The more Shelley learned about these options, the more she felt this was an opportunity to change the way we viewed our health in general. This foray into the natural health world triggered a personal transformation in me that was as powerful as any religious experience. As I began to understand the interconnectedness of my body, my

I calmed myself down, I entered a candlelit labyrinth, constructed to be used for prayer, meditation, and recollection of sin. The labyrinth was a catalyst for me—I had beautiful, metaphorical thoughts about my sin and stumbling blocks. Everyone gathered upstairs for singing, corporate profession of sin, prayer, and ashes. My Catholic background has made the acknowledgement of sin a very important aspect of my spiritual experience, and the beautiful gathering moved me. Sometime during the gathering I had an epiphany that I have not been confessing my sins since I've come to Solomon's Porch. I'm not sure what to do about that.

During lunch we got into a discussion about my aunt's chiropractor, who has spiritual gifts of healing, which he uses at Christian centers. I have been told that I have these same gifts and was very interested in his experience. I am very confused about how to use these gifts right now, after a very frightening experience with a healing art that I thought was harmless energy work but turned out to be spirit invoking. (Praise God for people in my church community who questioned this healing, and through whom I discovered the dangers of it!!!) The chiropractor has had no training in this healing, but treated his patients in the same way I did, by using his intuition to guide his hands, which were burning hot, to the right place. I think I should try to talk to him and other energy workers who are Christian. I want to use my gifts to help people, and I

emotions, and my mental health, I noticed changes in the way I understood the world. I no longer thought of my body as a separate entity housing my mind or spirit (something a theologically trained pastor certainly should have known, right?). I saw myself as a whole person. I found, though, that the kind of faith I had been living had little to say about this kind of holistic view of the self. In fact, during the early days of our involvement in the natural health world, we had concerns that it might lead us into non-Christian understandings and teachings. As it turned out nothing could have been further from our actual experience.

Over the last seven years the things I thought were dangerous have proven to be among the most useful insights and understandings I've found for living in the way of Jesus. There's a saying in natural health circles that I've found to be quite helpful in understanding the integrated life of faith: "Don't say that your hand hurts, as if your hand were something separate from you. Rather, say that you hurt in your hand." Even though it sounds like something from an episode of *Kung Fu* or *The Matrix* (not to mention Paul's letter to the church at Corinth), the idea behind this is that you're not separate from your own hand. You cannot remove yourself from your hand and speak of it as another thing with a pain that is unrelated to the rest of your body. If there is pain in the hand, there is pain in the body, there is pain in you. I've come to see that the same is true of the relationship between the body and the spirit. Anyone who has suffered from chronic pain knows that it goes far beyond a physical experience. Physical sensations affect us emotionally and spiritually because the body, the mind, and the soul are connected. Our desire to expand our expressions of faith in physical ways and to use physicality as a means of spiritual formation plays a role in nearly every practice of our community. Gathering together in a room on Sunday night somehow feels like the right way to act as a community. We need to be face to face, listening to each other sing and speak and pray.

I'm not sure that technology has been particularly helpful to churches in this area. Receiving spiritual formation online or from a sermon tape in the car may be convenient, but these versions of "church" pale in comparison to the physical act of entering a worship space with our community, seeing each other, touching each other, even being distracted by each other. When Jesus said, "Where two or more are gathered, I will be there among you," I think he was talking about more than his own presence. Jesus' call was not that we simply think together *about* him, it was a call to be together *with* him.

It shouldn't be surprising, then, that communion is a central element of our weekly gatherings. In some ways, it is communion, not the sermon, that is the centerpiece of our time together. Communion serves not only as a time of remembrance, but also as a full-body participatory experience. We believe that there is something greater going on than a group of people going through an act of remembering. We see the breaking of the body and shedding of blood through the lens of the physical resurrection. We are Easter people, celebrating the blessing of the resurrection.

It is to engage our bodies that communion has an interactive feel to it, with stations set around the room where people serve one another flavorful bread, juice, and wine. We seek to live reconciled lives with one another, so it's important to us that we serve the bread and the drink of communion to one another, offering ourselves to one another as expressions of peace and wholeness. Those who find meaning in the tradition of the common cup hold the cup for each other and drink of the same wine. In the serving, taking, and eating of the bread and drink we not only engage our thoughts and memories, but we also call into play our hands, our voices, our taste buds, our saliva, our digestive tracts. We all eat and drink together, and we hold hands and read the doxology from the book of Jude. In these ways we allow our entire bodies to take part in communion.

Truthfully, this is sometimes a little awkward. Our hands sometimes get sticky from a bit of spilled juice, or there might be a "bump" when two people reach for the same chunk of bread. Because we've been milling around, a lot of us may still have full-sized cups in our hands and bread in our mouths when it's time to hold hands with those around us. We may have to negotiate this hand holding. People will often be looking around for a place to set their cup, or quickly finishing their bread. We could build in a little more time or find other ways to eliminate this awkwardness, but I'm actually quite fond of it. I see it as part of people entering into the physical moment of holding another person's hand. There is tremendous value in letting go of one thing intentionally in order to take hold of something else.

PRAYER AND MEDITATION

One of the most exciting aspects of this pursuit of physical expressions of faith is the use of the body as a means of prayer. It's fascinating to me that physical postures—kneeling, raising our arms, placing our palms up—can lead our thoughts into a deeper state of prayer and meditation. In this process, the mind comes under the reign of the body in a way that cannot be forced but seems to come from a genuine connectedness between what we do and what we think.

am sure that God gave them to me for that purpose, so I am praying for wisdom and discernment about how to do this in the best and holiest way.

4-10-03
I thought a lot about physicality as I learned about the lymphatic and endocrine systems in my anatomy lecture and lab today. The more I learn about the human body, the more I am convinced that it is too intricate to have been created by anything except God. We have so many systems that are constantly subconsciously regulated. Our bodies have a natural intelligence and an amazing ability to heal themselves. I feel privileged to be entering a profession that helps return the body to its inherent, God-given intelligence.

DUSTIN

Every week presents itself like a buffet, each Tuesday evening with new tantalizing options. Tonight, it's the first night of Ad League Bowling at Stardust Lanes. And, man, Stardust has the best freakin' burgers in town. Serious grease fix with some of the best fries in town. Your colon will seize up like a heroin dance party. But that's not even the reason I skip tonight.

In the last 15 months, I've made a conscious effort to keep sane by balancing mind, body, and spirit. That sounds so lame. Reading back over it, I cringe and choke on my own yuppie bile. If I had any sense, I'd stab my brain with a Q-Tip and swear to never talk that way again. But in reality it's true. I make much more effort to exercise three times a

Physical postures are not our only method of prayer; there are times when prayer is primarily accomplished though the words of the person leading us. But to be honest, this kind of prayer feels less effective for us as a community because it is an auditory experience where we are seeking to cancel out our other senses, and participate by thinking about being in agreement with the words being spoken. Using our bodies allows us other portals into the experience of prayer.

Rather than requiring that everyone do the same thing, we often give a list of options of how we can express ourselves physically as prayer. At times we ask that people in a certain part of the room take on a particular prayer posture. We often invite people to stand, sit, kneel, squat, lay down, raise hands, or even keep their eyes open, allowing these postures to be our true prayer. Our desire is that our prayers would become more than making speeches with our eyes shut; it's much harder to fake a physical prayer than a spoken one. In using physical postures as prayer, we find that prayer becomes for us an elemental outgrowth of our efforts to live as blessings in the world.

During the most recent war in Iraq we asked everyone to face in the direction of Iraq and assume postures of healing, of safety, of peace. Some people knelt, some stood, some held their hands out in front of them as though straining to touch the people living with war. We prayed through a list of countries around the world where war and strife rage on, and yet these words were the context, not the crux of our prayer. It was in our turning, our reaching, our prostration that our real prayers were offered.

I recently organized a time of prayer at a convention of 1,100 church leaders. The prayer followed a powerful video presentation on AIDS in Africa, with a special focus on the children affected by this horrible disease. As I walked to the stage to lead the prayer, I sensed that no set of words, no matter how well crafted, would have allowed us to enter into this plight in a meaningful way.

Instead of using words to pray, I divided the room into four groups. The group on the right was invited to kneel as an act of prayer, submission, and solidarity for parents and children who mourn the loss of family members to AIDS. The people on the left were invited to stand on behalf of those so weakened by this terrible disease that they cannot stand on their own. The people in the back section were invited to raise their hands in a posture of begging for healing. Anyone who wished was invited to move to the aisles and dance for those who cannot dance in this world but will dance when all is remade.

This speechless prayer continued on for a long time. It was true prayer entered into with our bodies and hardly a word spoken. Here, as in our experience on Sunday evenings at Solomon's Porch, our bodies took us to places that words alone scarcely could. It also reinforced my conviction that we followers of Jesus must take part in alleviating this horrible epidemic lest we lose all moral credibility to assert that we are truly followers of God. We dare not continue to outsource this issue to government agencies or rock stars.

- - -

JAVIER

2.17.2003

Things with the pregnancy are good, and we are excited to be having a baby.

My life continues to be hard (come to think of it, I should have my own telethon). Stuck between feeling excitement and the feeling of "Wow, I am a father" isn't such a good place right now. I think I will probably remain there for the rest of my life... for some reason after hearing the sound of our baby's heartbeat I know that things will be all right because God is going to take care of us.

3.5.2003

I am still trying to figure out what I should give up for Lent. I have toyed with the idea of giving up playing guitar and writing songs, and yesterday I was joking with Naomi that I was going to give up Christianity. I figure that if we are going to give up something, it better be something that will cost us something.

That is why I like the church calendar. There is regularity to reminders that we will return to ashes, that there is a Kingdom with a King, and that this King is good.

3.6.2003

Today is Ash Wednesday and I am excited that for the first time we are having an ash service at SP. I think it is an amazing experience during and afterwards. I think it is the only time of the year where people leave church physically altered. They either forget to wipe their foreheads or just leave it on for some reason, but I sort of like to see people with ash on their forehead. It seems to me that it is like the tongues of fire that people saw during Pentecost.

Then the ash on the forehead came, which is an amazing experience to take part in. It connects so many things in Christianity for me. You have the previous year's palm leaves that are burned to make the ash, and then you have the anticipation of this year's resurrection and the whole time you wonder how much longer we must endure all the bad in life to get to the "good stuff." I think it is the whole Christian story in its most basic terms. We look back to what has already happened, we are in the middle of stuff right now doing the best we can, and we anticipate what is to come. The beautiful part to me of the whole thing is that the

week and keep on some sort of mental flexing regimen. Which is tough lately with Joe Millionaire and other reality shows waiting to atrophy my brain.

I head to the gym, hoping to catch some of God's beauty delivered in spandex and blonde pigtails. No such luck. I wish my gym had more lady members, but at the same time I don't need any more girl pressure while I'm covered in sweat and wearing my bright yellow Cliff's Notes T-shirt. I'm sure the day is coming when some coed bounces up to me while I'm benching 60 and professes her love for literary cheats and beer guts.

After an hour and change at the gym I head home to scrounge up some dinner. I prepare something quick. The Ash

Wednesday service is at 7:30. It will be the first service I have ever attended. I grew up in a Baptist setting where very little emphasis was put on the Lent season. It was always viewed as the time that "Catholics gave up something."

I'm impressed by the way the church smashes together so many denominations and says, "We have something to learn from lots of places." This meshing makes a gathering where Catholics worship next to Protestants and so forth. Something I have never really experienced.

Since I have no benchmark for how Ash Wednesday services should go, tonight's went well. From the beginning the mood for the evening was humility. Right away they ushered us through

story of Jesus is retold every year. And even if we may not fully understand, we must realize that Jesus didn't call us to understand as much as he called us to follow and do the things he did.

Sarah wasn't able to go to the gathering, so I took some ashes with me and placed them on her forehead when I got home. I also took some ashes and placed them on her belly for our baby.

Anyway, I like it because it sort of feels like a song. You know the part of a song where the build starts to happen, and you know the chorus is coming soon, and the tension of the song will soon be setting you free...That is what these days of Lent feel like to me.

5/19

So there it was. I was going to have my first experience with acupuncture. I don't know much about acupuncture except some stuff about it being too related to Eastern religions for any good Christian to have anything to do with it. Since on my best days I barely feel like a Christian, and much less a good Christian, I was more than excited to jump into the world of acupuncture.

The session was intense. It was a very interesting experience to feel energy flow from point to point in my body. It was very relaxing, too, so much that I fell asleep. I mentioned this to the lady that was poking me with the needles, and she said that I must have gone into a trance. Of course being one who has never experienced a trance, I can't tell you if I did or I didn't.

All kidding aside, though, I did feel like I was floating, and I did fall asleep. And from what I was telling her I was feeling, the lady did tell me that I must be very tuned in to my energy. Always made me feel good to have someone recognize that. I think.

So I have another appointment this coming Friday to get more work done.

Her diagnosis was that I have a lot of heat in me, and that all that heat is drying up my blood, which has lead to the dry skin. So the plan is to try to bring the heat down by bringing my ying back into harmony with my yang. This whole way of living life fascinates me.

I left with most of my belief system intact and, in fact, found a new appreciation and awe of the human body as an unbelievably precise and miraculous thing. The whole experience actually strengthened my faith. I find it incredible that people with a different belief system are helping me to discover new things about my faith.

CROSSING

During a recent Life Development Forum we offered a session on Christian practices. In one of the four weeks we introduced the act of making the sign of the cross on ourselves. This gesture has become a very powerful experience for me. It is rich with meaning and history and is such a simple way to proclaim and pray my faith with my body. I hold the fingers on my right hand in the shape of a cross, my index finger lying over the top of my outstretched thumb. I use the Eastern Orthodox pattern of touching first head, then heart, then right lung followed by left. Others in the group follow the Roman Catholic practice with left before right. I repeat words that we adapted from Paul's letter to the church in Colossae: "Jesus, may your cross be my cross and your life be my life." This is not superstition. It is a posture of prayer and faith that I desire to burn true in my life.

ANOINTING WITH OIL

The tradition of anointing with oil represents the presence and blessing of God. We honor this ancient practice of physical faith with the youngest of our community. We initiate new babies into our family of faith by anointing. Oil is applied to the child's head, the side of her eyes, mouth, ears, chest, hands, feet, and knees. A prayer of blessing is prayed: "God, may this child have your wisdom in her mind, her eyes see your glory, her ears hear your voice, her mouth tell your truth, her heart be your home, her hands do your work, her feet follow wherever you lead, and her knees only bow before her loving Lord and God." Through this prayer all are reminded of the ways in which our bodies are to be used in faithful acts of worship and service.

EASTER AND THE BODY

At Solomon's Porch, the physical nature of the incarnation and resurrection spurs us to create practices in which our bodies help us to follow Jesus. The Easter season, then, is a natural time to incorporate new physical elements into our community life; there is no better way to tell the story of the physical suffering, death, and resurrection of Jesus than with our own bodies.

The first day of Lent this year brought the first Ash Wednesday gathering in our church's history and in mine. The evening began with people walking a candlelit labyrinth Luke had designed and laid out in the kitchen. The experience of walking a labyrinth invites the body into a rhythm of moving around and moving toward the center, then back out. Dozens of people may walk the labyrinth together, some walking in, some walking out. That means moving our bodies in ways to pass one another and accommodate another person's moments of still reflection. This is not at all a mindless act but a conscious physical engagement.

a prayer labyrinth with meditative music in the background. Just coming from the gym I had a really hard time settling down and focusing. I eventually kicked the trip enough to have meditative prayer and make it through the maze. In the labyrinth I focused on Daniel's prayer in chapter 2. I asked God for forgiveness for not knowing how to pray and yet, as he has done before, give me the wisdom to pray a bit better.

Tonight at the Ash Wednesday service I just tried to incorporate the crying kids into my worship. Much like outside is full of distractions and other things vying for my attention, I had to work that much harder to focus on the important things. And focus I did. Doug did a great job moving us through an evening of repentance and admission of guilt. We sang and prayed together with the evening capped off with a "laying of ash" or something like that.

Now the whole marking the sign of the cross on the forehead with last year's burnt palm leaves is kinda weird. For a Baptist with minimal pre-Easter training, I'm still digesting. When I got the ash applied, all I could think was that "God was a citronella candle."

SARAH

3/11

I am tired today. Not so much physically, but more mentally. I'm tired of so much. I wish I could take a week off of life and just be. It would be nice to stop for awhile. But it seems that the older I get, the more complicated my life becomes. More things and people are added,

It involves introspection, consideration, desire, and physical movement all coming together in a brief communal pilgrimage. On this night, the center point was used for quiet reflection.

As people completed the labyrinth, we proceeded upstairs for a time of corporate confession and the application of ashes. Until this point, Ash Wednesday had not been part of my Christian faith experience. Not only had I never applied ashes to anyone's forehead, but I had also never had them applied to mine. After this experience I wondered how I could have celebrated 19 Easters as a Christian without this tremendous experience. It was such a powerful moment to kneel, to be marked physically with the ashes of my mortality, and to confess the faith, and I was overcome with emotion again while applying ashes to these wonderful people who wanted so much for their faith to be on, in, and through their bodies.

A month later, during Easter week, we celebrated a full Passover meal on Wednesday night. The explanation of the elements of the Passover meal not only brought deeper understanding of Passover and communion, but it also highlighted the deeply physical stories of the exodus of the nation of Israel from Egypt and the crucifixion of Jesus. The meal, which took hours to finish, was a full-body experience of moving about, tasting, smelling, singing, and digesting. We were listening to words and to our bodies as we ingested foods that serve a symbolic purpose as well as a physical one. The spiritual and the physical were not separate aspects of this meal but one and the same.

On Maundy Thursday, the day before Good Friday, we lived the story of the disciples being asked to stay awake with Jesus by holding an all-night prayer vigil. The vigil began with a time of prayer led by nine people, most of whom had very little church experience and certainly no experience with being part of a liturgical religious processional. Dan bore a Bible over his head as a sign of his commitment to live under the authority of the faith. Janelle carried a lighted candelabra in token that Jesus is the light of the world. Rachel brought in the wine of bitter rejection and of spilled blood. Josh carried the cross of his Lord. Thom, who was deep in the pain of a just-finalized, unwanted divorce, led communion and invited us to join in with this reconciliatory sacrifice of Jesus.

Then people came to the church in half-hour shifts to sit at the altar of repose and keep watch over the cup and the bread. Again, the act of holding off sleep, of staying awake when the body aches for rest, is a deeply physical expression of worship and faithfulness.

Good Friday evening offered an extraordinary event we called "The Way of the Cross." It was a collaborative art experience depicting each station of the cross in a visual medium and a performance medium. The story was told not simply with words but through art created with hands, dance, and poetry worked out through limbs and lungs, music played with fingers and feet.

On Saturday we gathered in various homes to live that day as the disciples might have—we ate simple meals together and reflected on the disciples' confusion, sadness, and attempts to return to their regular lives. In physically coming together, we were making the day between Good Friday and Easter Sunday part of the story of Jesus.

On Easter morning we gathered at Powderhorn Park at 6 a.m., just as the sun was rising, to tell the story of the risen Lord. That story always seems to have more significance when it is told in the cool morning air, accompanied by the slight burn of tired eyes. We then enjoyed a celebration breakfast at Marc and Alicia Belton's home.

Putting all of this together was a tremendous amount of work—in all, there were nearly 100 people taking part in some aspect of these celebrations and gatherings. And yet there is something very right about the Easter season being all-consuming, about it taking our time and our energy. The death and resurrection of Christ should take the wind out of us. It should get in the way of our meals and our sleep and our plans. It should absorb every other aspect of our lives so that nothing we do can happen without being thought of in the context of Easter. In living this season with our bodies, our community was able to dive deeper into the way of Christ.

MASSAGE

I'd like to introduce you to Marlene, who has been part of our community since the beginning and who uses a room in our building for her massage therapy work. Maybe it's the Enya music or maybe it's the New Age influences on massage that have made this practice suspect in some Christian circles. But the work Marlene does as a massage therapist is part of the spiritual formation that happens in our community.

I've been practicing massage therapy out of our church for about two years now.

and no matter what, I never seem to be able to simplify things. People say life only becomes more chaotic when you have kids. Well, I'm having a kid. Sometimes I hardly think I can do all I've got now, and then I'm throwing a kid into the mix. The thing is, I know that all I need to do is learn to find peace no matter what my circumstances, but that is easier said than done. Sometimes I feel like I'm praying myself blue in the face asking God for peace. And nothing happens. Life goes on. Still agitated. "Have faith," people say. "It'll come in God's time." Well, what if God's time includes the emotional destruction of me? Christians aren't exempt from crappy lives. I could be one of the many torn apart by their own humanity. So maybe I'm a little melodramatic and negative. I'm just tired of trying to find peace and faith. If God feeds the birds of the air and clothes the flowers of the field than he'll take care of us too… sure, but some of those birds get hit by cars, and some of those flowers die during a drought.

3/11
And then something as simple as a beautiful snowfall brings me hope again…

It has been a journey through my fundamental evangelical background even to do massage. Like many others, I associated Eastern medicine with Eastern religions such as Buddhism and needed to reconcile that in my head to make sure I wasn't going to fall into some weird spiritual practices. I laugh now at the fact that I was ever wigged out about doing massage. Now I realize that much of Eastern medicine is closer to the holistic model of faith I believe in than Western medicine. The relationship between the mind, body, and spirit makes more sense to me than the idea that they have little to do with one another.

It has been an honor, a joy, a mystery, a sacrament, and an expression of love to do massage for people, especially in the place our community uses for worship of God. I find God using massage to heal parts of people they might not have known needed healing. I also find that touching people in this way gives me a chance to offer God's care to people who might never open themselves to it in other ways. Larry came in for about his third visit. I usually start at the top of a person's head and work toward the feet. As I was beginning work on Larry's shoulders, he flinched. He told me, "It always takes me a moment to adjust to you touching me, Mar. There's nowhere else in my life that I have people touching me." It was a powerful and humbling moment for me to realize how many of us are walking around with the need to be touched in a right way and how often we are touched in the wrong ways, increasing our appetite for touch that is based on human respect and love and that can feed our souls.

Another client, who is part of our community and the victim of multiple sexual assaults, came in recently. I rarely feel like I do anything for her when she comes for a massage. Sometimes my desire to scoop her in my arms and run away to a place she can feel whole is barely controllable. But I know the thing that would truly save her would be to stay and ground her with love to help her through the pain. So I resign myself to meditate on her, keeping my hands on her, my feet on this earth, and connected to her by the only thing that will restore her, the love and grace of God.

I often do massage for other female victims of sexual assault at a shelter our church has supported. The impact of appropriate, healing touch on these women is astonishing. A woman I'll call Jean had "ghost pains," pain in places with no visible trauma (as veterans feel pain in an amputated limb). She felt pain to the touch all around her collarbone, a place I don't actually massage but do touch as I work other muscles. My plan was that over several massages I would come closer and closer to her collarbone, hopefully letting her build trust to the touch there and replacing those memories of painful touch. On about her fourth or fifth visit I didn't think I had come very close to it yet, but she jumped and grabbed my hand and motioned to me to give her a minute to collect herself and speak. I apologized and she settled herself enough to explain. When I'd touched her, she remembered something. When she was about eight, her mother pushed her down a flight of stairs. As she lay at the bottom in pain, she spotted her grandmother. Either verbally or with her eyes she remembers pleading for help. Her grandmother approached her, stood over her and stomped on her neck. Jean's head slammed into the cold, hard floor. The impression of the footprint apparently lasted for years. That day, Jean's grandmother kicked the door shut on Jean's personal prison. Hopefully that day in the massage we took the first step at unlocking it.

There are so many other memorable moments for me. I have done massages with pregnant mothers and shared grief with widows. I have used massage as a form of prayer, and I have used it with young teenage girls to define their bodies. I have used it as encouragement and stress relief for those in financial difficulties and saw one of my seated massage students perform probably the first massage ever for a single mother in our community. Most of my massages are perhaps not conscious forms of the physicality of God, but when I touch people, I can feel my hands soak into their backs. I feel the meditation of the comfort, the relief of the ache; I know the sense of refuge where peace comes over you and releases the stress from your body. I know it is breaking—sometimes shattering—the ghost wall that separates them from others. There is no hiding. I am in, and it is an honor to be there.

A DANGER ZONE?

Much has been written in recent years about the effect of the Enlightenment on Christianity, including the shift from a faith of the body to a faith centered in the mind, thought, and belief. As a result, many today question the appropriateness of a faith that is grounded in the physical world. In addition, a plethora of Christian literature warns the church in North America of the danger posed by the New Age and other Eastern ways of thinking and living.

This unease notwithstanding, the danger we face is less that Eastern world-views will unravel Christianity than that our Western perspectives will neuter our Christian faith. For Christianity was and is from Hebrew Eastern origins. Christianity is not a faith of the Western mind; it is a faith that was brought *to* the Western mind.

The church has so thoroughly given up acknowledging the role of the body in spirituality that many Christians mistakenly see this as the primary difference between Christianity and the New Age. Some even assert that Christianity is about the mind and the spirit while the New Age is about the body and the spirit.

What makes this so bizarre is that, when it comes to physical spirituality, the best transcendental meditation class can't hold a candle to the faith that proclaims the incarnation and bodily resurrection and the God Who is One.

We are a physical people when we follow Jesus. We are a people of a physical spiritual formation, one that neither degrades nor ignores the mind but that melds the emotional, the spiritual, and the physical ways of being formed as the people of the Savior.

Kingdom Come

Have I failed to notice cripples being healed?
Heaven's grace upon us, its mercy's been revealed.
There's no other name in heaven or on earth.
So who are we to hand out worth?

Chorus:
Kingdom come on earth as it is in heaven.
And have we learned to seek it in our lives?
We are born; inherited the darkness.
But as a child turn darkness into light.

Have you ever noticed all that's not quite real?
Bread without the crust; a ship without its keel,
Sleepless nights and a babe without its birth.
Along came the one who loved us first.

Kingdom come on earth as it is in heaven.
And have we learned to seek it in our lives?
We are born; inherited the darkness.
But as a child turn darkness into light.

A mustard seed, a bunch of yeast,
a treasure hidden in a field.
Who kneads the dough and sows the seed,
At harvest time His crop will yield.

Kingdom come on earth as it is in heaven.
And have we learned to seek it in our lives?
We are born; inherited the darkness.
But as a child turn darkness into light.

CHAPTER 05

SPIRITUAL FORMATION THROUGH DIALOGUE

TUESDAY

It is Tuesday evening, May 6, almost time for the Bible discussion group. (I admit that for a church of pretty artistic people, we don't have very creative titles for our happenings; we kind of like simple, straightforward names for things.) We meet each week from 7:30 to 9:30 p.m. to read and discuss the section of the Bible we'll be looking at during our Sunday gathering.

When I arrive at the building, Lisa is waiting in her car and steps out to meet me. Our attention quickly turns to the two young men who just pulled over to our side of the road. They are parked where two other guys parked a couple of Sundays ago to sell drugs from their car, and it seems to me the intentions of these two are the same. I let Lisa into the building and head back outside to make eye contact and let our "visitors" know that this is a street where people pay attention. As I walk around our front "yard" picking up garbage and generally making my presence known, I can't help but wonder if what we're about to do in the Bible discussion group has any real effect on this neighborhood. I know that our conversation will be of some value to those who show up, but what use is it to people who are victims and perpetrators of the pain that comes from illegal drug use and the poverty that so easily condones and supports it? Questions like these dog me as a pastor and keep me constantly reevaluating how we should go about living in the way of Jesus in this time and place.

Most Tuesday nights our group ranges in size anywhere from eight to 20 people. Tonight there are 14 of us, mostly regulars but with a sprinkling of newcomers. As with all of our community activities, this discussion is open to everyone.

To begin the Bible discussion, we always share our full names—first, middle, and last. Everyone does this, regulars and newcomers alike. This is partly by way of introduction and breaking the ice, but it also sends some important messages. First, we are more than our first names. The use of our middle and last names serves as a reminder that we come from families who gave us our names and have shaped the people we are as well as the beliefs we hold. Second, the com-

ERIN

3-9-03

In our Bible discussion time we finished the chapter of Daniel. Doug left us with a lovely question – how do we, as Christians, become more like Daniel and Esther and Ezra and want to become involved in stories like theirs, instead of extracting from their stories? I love that Solomon's Porch, on so many levels, really encourages people to get wrapped up in the things of God. Although I'm far from being the most active person at church, I feel more and more compelled to put as much time and energy into God and Solomon's Porch as my schedule will allow me to.

After church I had a great talk with Marlene, who has a gift of strong intuition and premonition. We have had multiple con-

ing discussion is to be people-centered, rather than only idea-centered. The full names remind us that, even when we do not care for someone's contributions, we are to behave with respect and dignity.

At this time each week everyone shares an answer to a lighthearted question, like their favorite candy or the name of their second-grade crush. These weird little tidbits go a long way toward helping us learn more about each other and see each other as complex human beings with a history of experiences. It's also a little hard to be too intimidated by someone who just told you she wishes she could still wear her moon boots. Most importantly these questions get people used to talking in the group and to hearing their own voices holding center court.

During our Sunday-night gatherings, we read through rather large sections of the Bible (like a chapter or two, sometimes more), so during the Bible discussion group we read the section aloud with each person reading as much as they want before letting someone else take over. We also try to read from a few different translations of the Bible so we get a deeper understanding. On this night, we actually pull out the Greek lexicon to find the root of a word that's puzzling to us, but it doesn't help much; as is often the case the English versions seem to do a more than adequate job for us. We talk about the issues raised, any elements that are confusing, and what the passage tells us about our role in God's story. The energy of the conversation moves from person to person as we share thoughts and ideas.

For some this is sort of an upside-down way of looking at the Bible. It's more common for a pastor or an individual to approach the Bible with a subject in mind and then search for what it has to say on that topic. But we've gotten amazing outcomes from gathering as a community and letting the Bible unfold and lead us.

That doesn't mean we just open the Bible and pick a place to read. Rather, we intend that the Bible function as a full member of our community; on every subject of which it speaks, we listen. Our discussions allow the Bible to come alive and speak much more passionately or emphatically than anything I could drum up on my own.

Tonight we're actually looking ahead a few weeks. After several weeks of reading through the book of Daniel, we're considering a three- or four-week tour through a New Testament book, but we haven't settled on which one. I have suggested Titus to the Bible discussion group, so we spend the night reading and discussing the first two chapters. By the end of the night, the consensus was to not go with Titus, and I was "commissioned" to consider going in another direction. It isn't that we don't like Titus, but that we feel the complicated story of church leadership that consumes much of the letter does not fit our situation for a Sunday-night gathering.

The Bible discussion group differs from a traditional Bible study. We aren't just getting together to read and extract from the Bible and deepen our own understanding. Rather, this group is like a microcosm of our community, standing in for others as we enter into the passage. In many ways this group sets the form and feel and content for what will happen on Sunday night during our worship gathering. Together we explore the questions and issues so that when the same passage is presented to the larger group, it will be clear that it has been wrestled with not just by the theologian who gives the sermon (me) but by "regular" people as well.

Wes is a 49-year-old computer analyst and Bible discussion group regular. Wes contributes during the discussion on Tuesday nights and continues thinking and adding to the dialogue on his own. Occasionally, as in this e-mail, he lets me in on his thinking process.

> Hi Doug,
>
> I think we had an enjoyable and interesting discussion which, as you commented, has a fairly limited application. Questions like, "Is this statement too culturally bound to be useful?" or "Do we know enough about the context to provide a balanced commentary?" These are important questions, but I'm afraid they became a little debilitating for us. I feel we found ourselves unable to identify the core issues the text itself is addressing to allow it to ask its questions of us.
>
> Generally, I think Titus is asking us, Do we have what it takes to flourish as a group? What sort of understandings, hopes, and dreams are driving the enterprise? What kinds of people need to be at the tiller? What kind of people should we be generally in order for the group to flourish? What kind of things need to be talked about so we can grow? Are we able to respond to adversaries with wisdom and steadfastness? Do we have adversaries (if not, why not?), and what do they look like?

versations attempting to sort out how to best use these gifts in a Christian way. We have certainly not come to any conclusions about how to do that, but we think we may be getting close to knowing why God gives us these thoughts. God gives us premonitions so that we can take appropriate action. Sometimes I feel like God really lets me know what he wants me to do, and I should feel really blessed.

15 March 2003
I got into a great discussion with Shelley about sin and my newly realized need to confess it. A lot of women had amazing ideas about how we can confess our sin individually. A beautiful idea was to write sins in a garden of sand in the prayer room, then leaving them there for someone else to pray for and then erase. Another

I think we could almost have another Bible discussion group about this, a little more creative about the themes and meanings and less analytical. But I'm still not sure we need to actually do Titus right now. Maybe the issues aren't compelling for us. I'll be supportive of any decision. I hope this helps.

Wes Johnson

Each week around 9:30, we end with someone offering a paraphrase of John 14:25-26, in which Jesus says, "All this I have spoken while still with you. But the Counselor, the Holy Spirit, whom the Father will send in my name, will teach you all things and will remind you of everything I have said to you." We trust the Holy Spirit as the arbiter and teacher of truth during our time together, so with this prayer we ask that the Spirit would keep in our minds things said that accord with the ways and teachings of Jesus.

Our formal business is done, but people continue to talk as I shut the door and set the alarm.

As I head for my Buick about 9:45, I notice that the "small business" by the road has moved on. Getting into my car, I wonder if they just closed shop early—or if what we did tonight may have had an effect after all. Who knows?

...

WHY WE TALK ABOUT THE BIBLE

The Bible discussion group is my primary time of preparation for the following Sunday's sermon, not only because it gives me a better idea of how to focus what I'm going to say, but also because I like the idea of the sermon being something more than just my thoughts and research on a passage. Part of our desire is to be a community that is equipped to contribute to the future thinking, life, and faith of the Church. This means we need to not only hear the thoughts of those who have gone before us, but also to create new ways of thinking and living the dreams and ways of God.

I feel very blessed to join bright, insightful, and informed people on Tuesday nights, but I think there's something more going on than just an interesting discussion. On Tuesday nights something is created in the dynamics of the group as we listen to one another, wander down the roads of the thoughts of others, and allow the Bible to contribute fully to the discussion. We aren't people simply listening or talking. We are people entering into the story of God's work in the world and seeking our place in that story.

This process helps me see the passage as a living testament with much to say to us in the here and now. It allows me to go into Sunday knowing that I am not just a guy spewing out my "vast" knowledge of the Bible, but a member of a community who is being formed on the spot by the God-given insights of others—in short, a member of a dialogue.

Dialogue has become something of a lost art in Christianity. As worship has shifted from the New Testament description of life-on-life faith to the speaker/audience model used by many churches, we've moved away from using dialogue as a means of spiritual formation.

But I've found that for many people, especially those who learn by talking and don't fully know what they believe until they hear themselves say it, dialogue offers a stream of hope toward a new, deeper kind of life with God.

Dialogue isn't just helpful in spiritual formation, it may be essential. If people are to center their lives on the story and call of Jesus, we as the church need to find ways to help the truths of Jesus become embedded in those lives. For many people, that can only happen when they are allowed to turn an idea over in their heads for a while, to ask questions of it, to make sense of it in their own time and in light of their own experiences.

Anna, another of the Tuesday-night regulars, recently noted that she's often struggled with more traditional religious teaching. "During a sermon," she says, "I feel like my job is to just sit there and take it." For her, participating in a dialogue about the difficult questions and demands of faith has meant the difference between being an active player in the story of God and being the passive recipient of someone else's ideas. There is no question which approach Anna would choose.

In every communication process there are at least two authors, the one generating or expressing the idea and the one rebirthing the idea in her or his own mind. A person who simply listens to a speech or sermon really isn't given time to process the ideas—by the time the idea is out there, the presenter has moved on to the next thought.

cussion. I am constantly amazed at how differently people think and how enlightening it can be to hear others' points of view. For instance, Wes said that he has wasted time in the past questioning that God loves him. Luke said that the question he would ask instead is about the authenticity of the Bible because if it is true, then God definitely loves us. My personal hang-up hasn't been about questioning God's love for me but rather if I love him enough, or if I am serving him well enough.

DUSTIN

I haven't been to a Bible discussion group in over a year. I stopped going because I really felt like I wasn't getting anything out of it I didn't just get by reading my Bible's footnotes and praying about the passages. This week, *however, we're reading Daniel, and "Shoot Gene," it's some tough stuff. The whole stuff about the good angel getting held up by the bad angel really was like a bad trip. I needed someone else to help me wade through that whole "end of the world as we know it" thing. Plus I needed to get that R.E.M. song out of my head.*

After the "feel-good share moment" we turned to Daniel and read the final four chapters. Marcus piped in, "Now what? Any thoughts?" An hour and a quarter later we had come to the same prophetic ideas that I came with that evening. Daniel is one confusing mo'fo. I was jones'n for answers, and all I got was a head game. We called it a game after another half-hour, but I left feeling no more

Doesn't it seem strange that when we're talking about the life-transforming process of a person being captured by the story of God, we fail to make room for true two-way conversation?

My wife and I used an illustration of the importance of conversation in communication at a marriage retreat we recently facilitated (the idea isn't original to us, by the way). It works like this:

A couple sits back to back. In front of each of them is a table with a set of building blocks. With the sets, which are identical, each is to build the same structure. One person is the instructor, and the other must do as instructed. But while the instructor gives orders to match what he is doing—"Lay the long blue one on its side. Place the small yellow arc on the end" and so on—the other partner has to remain silent. No questions, no clarification, nothing. Invariably, when the spouses see what the other has made, they discover their projects look nothing alike. Then they redo the exercise, but this time both partners can communicate, asking as many clarifying questions as they like. As you can imagine, this time the structures they make are nearly identical.

It's obvious where I'm going with this. One-way communication leaves people frustrated. The result of such communication rarely satisfies the speaker or the hearer. No matter how often we do it or what visual support we use, lecture is just plain poor communication compared to dialogue.

AVOIDING HERESY

If discussion is a primary means of spiritual formation, how do we handle those times when people say things not in agreement with what the church has held to throughout the ages? In other words, how do we handle heresy?

As I mentioned, we commit ourselves to the guidance of the Holy Spirit in the belief that with that guidance will come discernment and the ability to recognize truth. If someone in our community says something that's totally off base and is clearly their own creation, someone else might say, "Well, that's an interesting thought. I've never heard anything like that before." We then try to gently call on our Christian traditions to help clarify why a certain kind of thinking isn't really consistent with orthodoxy. Alternatively, if someone presents a position that was held in the past but has been rejected by orthodox Christianity, then someone else who knows the issue will provide the necessary context.

In no case do we try to preempt every unwanted comment. For one thing, the censoring approach serves neither the originator of the idea, who may need to hear herself say it to know if she believes it, nor the listener, who may need to hear it before he determines that he doesn't hold to it. The protection from wrong belief comes from having an integrated and involved community of people who engage in one another's lives, not from limiting what is presented. People in our information-frenzied world have developed very effective ways of filtering input. We are used to judging new thoughts and allowing them to have authority in our lives or not to. So no one is going to just accept another's comment blindly—not even mine.

Part of our comfort with this approach is the realization that our communal understanding of faith and God cannot be unraveled by someone getting up and saying something goofy for four minutes.

The truth of the matter is that we all hold beliefs that are heretical or goofy to one degree or another. Being in a community where we discuss our beliefs and thoughts allows us to see our own more clearly. We are not left to ourselves to obtain right belief, nor are we given the impression that only a select few members of the body can be trusted to instruct us in the ways of faith.

For those who find little struggle in life and faith, dialogue may seem like a very unproductive, tangent-ridden waste of time. But those for whom struggle is a constant companion find in dialogue a crucial practice of faith. Wes pointed this out recently in commenting on his upbringing in a faithful Christian home. In his family, the goal of spiritual formation was that a person would know precisely what should be known. There was little room for dialogue. Anyone who disagreed with the "correct" position was seen as the opposition and was likely to be attacked. Wes says he enjoys the Bible discussion group and Solomon's Porch because they model working through struggle—not just the struggle with ideas, but with turning those ideas into a thoughtful, intentional life in the way of Jesus.

It seems to me there is a larger societal benefit in becoming a people of conversation, in learning to listen to those with whom we disagree. We live in a world that is increasingly separated and fragmented; we are able to live comfortably in circles in which everyone agrees with us. This is comfortable and easy—but it does not make for good Kingdom living. We are all called to learn from and listen to those who would challenge us and not just those who agree with us.

enlightened than when I came. But that's just it. Some weeks will be clear beacons from God with clarity and connection not derived from this earth, but other nights will be like tonight. Tough material with a tough crowd. It's only after wading through weeks of ups and downs that a rhythm starts to develop. I just wish I put my foot back in the pool on an up week and didn't have to have to work at believing that it was just an off week.

Regardless of how the evening went, I have been focusing on this part of the Bible in my own time and have felt a bit of an understanding. As basic as some of the stuff is, this part of the Bible has challenged the way I pray and perceive the future. Almost a "pray for grace and the will of God, because I can't possibly understand what is 'right' or not in this world."

JIM
1/30/03
Last night at the Wednesday night community meal about 10 of us sat around the dinner table. Conversations were happening everywhere, and as usual I gravitated toward Doug because I think he understands me better than anyone even though we barely know each other. At least he understands my faith struggle. During the conversation we discussed current U.S. warmongering by the politicians and how carefully words are chosen in politics to keep people happy. Ironically it caused me to remember a question someone asked of Doug during last week's sermon response time. "Is it your belief that Jesus

This isn't simply a move toward being more tolerant people but toward being salt and light in the world. How can we bless the lives of others without a willingness to engage in conversation with them?

It's important to note that a dialogue is not a debate; for dialogue to be effective, we need to resist the urge to cut people off and fix what they say. Healthy dialogue involves entering into the reality of the other. Our hope at Solomon's Porch is that our practice of healthy dialogue will not end as we leave our meetings or gatherings but will form new habits in us and make us into new people.

Forming new ways is often difficult. Spiritual formation through dialogue is hard work. Sometimes the discussion following the sermon goes down a different path than I had hoped and in my opinion becomes less than useful. Sometimes people share observations that are not particularly helpful. There have even been occasions when people have used the discussion to take us to task for issues all of which are not even legitimate. It can be excruciating to sit there and just listen—not only for me as a pastor but also for us as a community. We are forced to listen as well as talk. We are forced to consider ideas that are not our own and may never be. We are forced to live openly and graciously within a community of people we might not always agree with. Let me assure you this is much harder work than delivering a well-crafted message.

In dialogue you are not allowed to stay right where you are; you must move toward the perspective of the other person. You don't need to stay there, but a commitment to community means that you are required to visit.

It's also become clear to me that dialogue works best when it's face to face. Many of the people in our community are part of the "wired" generation, comfortable with technology and young enough not to remember life before computers and the Internet. When we set up our Web site, I expected our online bulletin board and chat rooms to fill up quickly—but, outside of specifically orchestrated efforts, both our boards and our chat areas have been complete failures.

This failure could be something specific to our community, but my hunch is that cyber-community just isn't as satisfying as person-to-person conversation. Given a choice between a personal conversation and a virtual one, most people would rather see the tears, hear the laughter, hold the hand. People like to be heard, they like to have a voice, they want to make an impact and be impacted by others. Dialogue allows those things to happen.

JAVIER

3.7.2003

Today I had a guy tell me that he and his pastor had handed out a bag full of tracts at the Minnesota State High School hockey tournament. He was proud that he did that, and I am sure he felt that he had fulfilled something that God wants us to do. I have been on the giving and receiving end of these little pamphlets, and having been on both sides, I can say they are for the most part an utter waste of time. Don't get me wrong; I am a wholehearted proponent of telling people the story of the gospel. I just think that giving someone you have never met a pamphlet and saying something like "Here, take this and read it when you have the time" doesn't amount to much in the way of retelling any stories, much less telling the story of redemption.

If you are going to take the time to give someone a little pamphlet with the words '"Secret to Life," please at least have the courtesy to talk to them and dialogue with them. And if you are out eating and are even thinking about leaving one, let me save you the mental anguish you will go through.....you are just wasting your time.

3.13.2003

On Tuesday I was able to go to the Bible discussion group. It was good to go because I haven't been able to go for several months. We discussed the passages in Matthew and Luke that deal with Christ being baptized and then being sent to the wilderness to be tempted by the devil. There were many different angles that people brought up, which I think is one of the benefits of being involved in a group like that. Most of us, be it through education or experience, already have our predetermined biases, and it is good to have someone else help you step away from those and see from another perspective.

3.3.2003

While we were at a maternity store, I picked up a book about how to teach a boy to become a man. It was one of those books where there is a single clever remark per page. I thought it would be fun to read it to pass the time while Sarah was getting some stuff. After reading it for a while, I was fighting back tears. I was reading all these one-sentence statements, and everything inside of me wished that these things had been done for me. Then I got to wondering how much different of a man I would be now had some of those things been done for me by a father. Then I began to wonder if I would succeed in doing some of those things for our child.

Maybe it is because sometimes I don't feel much like a man that these feelings came out. Half the time I feel like a teenager stuck inside the body of a 28-year-old, hoping that no one will find out that I am not who I say I am.

Then I start to wonder about the validity of something I read a year or so ago in a book by John Eldridge. Basically, he said that as you are growing up, the men in your life pass on manhood to you. That one day they look at you and tell you that you are now a man, and from that day forward they treat you as such and do all the "man stuff" with you.

Being a man is a hard thing, and there are few examples to follow.

really said that?" I realized that Doug is very much in the role of a politician. People are constantly waiting for him to screw up, to say the thing that confirms their belief that he is "leading us astray" or out of "orthodoxy." I told Doug that it's for this reason that I don't think I could be a pastor. I'd have no patience to do anything but lay on the line what I think about things. Why should I sit back and listen to some line of thinking that I think is either harmful or narrow and not lay out a way of thinking that I believe is consistent with the story of Jesus that I know? Why not challenge people's thinking? I'm starting to believe that I'm doing a disservice if I don't share with others some of the things that have dramatically impacted my life and saved my faith.

CARLA

1/30/03

One of the struggles I've had at SP has been a nagging sense of loneliness. One of the aspects of my depression is that I have a hard time figuring out how to connect with people. I don't really know how to get to know people, how to break through the chit-chat level. I'm also extra sensitive to feeling left out of the relationships I see around me. I think, "Why don't they want to get to know me?"

But over the last few weeks, people have begun to approach me. A few weeks ago Colleen asked if we could get together just to talk. I was scared to death to call her, not because of her, but because it's so hard for me to venture into friendships. But finally, I did it and we met for coffee. We did-n't talk about any-

Most men I know are either enthralled with work, some sort of self-enlightenment crap, or getting with a woman. Very few are taken with the thought of living a full life in search of adventure or danger. I don't know, maybe I have a romanticized view of what being a man means, but I just know that there is something inside of me that cringes at the thought of guys who are not passionate about things that matter – a cause.

I wonder at SP how we are going to transfer manhood to the boys there...

I also wonder what we are teaching about being men...

3/3

Last Monday my car finally died, and I didn't have the energy to deal with it anymore, so on Tuesday I put an ad in the weekly e-mail letting people know that I am looking for an inexpensive car. Part of me didn't think people actually read the weekly e-mail, but apparently they do because that afternoon I got an e-mail from Erin Anderson (the same Erin who is also doing the journaling thing for this book) and she told me of a car she had for sale because she had gotten a car from her grandmother. To make a long story short, I am now driving a '95 Honda Civic. It runs really well, and I hope it stays like that for a long time.

WHO'S IN CHARGE?

It can be nerve-racking for a pastor to give up being the one who decides what gets said and taught in a community. But after three years of weekly discussion groups and dialogues following my sermons, I've found that people— even those who are new to things of faith—really do know a lot about the Bible and the implications of the story of God in their lives.

As part of our sermon time on Sunday nights, we open up the discussion to anyone with comments, reflections, views, even dissension about what's been said. For first-time visitors, this is one of the more distinctive elements of our worship gathering, and oddly, newcomers often join right in the discussion. But from my perspective this dialogue isn't so much my sermon followed by a Q&A session. I think of the sermon itself as a discussion involving our community, the Bible, those who have come before us, and those around the world who seek the same goal of living lives faithful to the way of Jesus. Our sermons are not primarily about extracting truth from the Bible and applying those realities to people's lives. Rather we are trying to allow the world we live in and the faith we hold to interact, to dance, to inform each other. We can't do that if I'm the only one who gets to talk.

When I talk, I often use the phrase "it seems to me." This is an important discipline for me to practice and for my listeners to hear. It reminds both of us that what I'm saying is really just my take on things. There are times when I'm quite convinced of the position I'm expressing, but regardless of my level of conviction, it's still my take on things, which is influenced by all kinds of factors—my experiences, my education, my past. I am hopeful that the posture of an "it seems to me" attitude is one of invitation. It invites others to hold my same position, but doesn't demand that they do so. There is nothing soft, weak, or relative about recognizing that my beliefs are just that, beliefs. While I hold many of them for really good reasons, they are not unarguable professions. A good conversation will almost certainly make this clear.

When people see that their input and their thoughts matter, we become a community where people feel encouraged and called to share in other ways.

Marlene, who has been part of community from the beginning and is a consummate dialoguer, recently asked people on her e-mail list to reflect on where they have seen God's activity in their lives. The following are excerpts from some of the responses:

In the spirit of things going on in my life and the gathering last night: "Where have you see God, and what did that look like?"

----Original Message Follows----

From: Mike Rafferty

I'd like to finish my story shared at the gathering last evening. The one about the neighbor lady who has been repeatedly victimized by graffiti vandalism. After she used my mobile phone to call a relative to come over, she handed me the phone and said (and I quote), "Isn't God great?" That was the whole point of the story (it wasn't about me or the mobile phone or anything else).

So I have been thinking since that, as people from the neighborhood filter in over time, wouldn't it be grand if we would offer to neighborhood Porchers a hand painting over the graffiti? We could do it in late fall when it is cooler on a weekend day or two. If anyone is interested, please run with it, and I will gladly help out (no idea what my time commitments will be this summer and fall).

----Original Message Follows----

thing earth-shattering, but she was easy to talk to, and we laughed a lot, which, for me, is a great foundation for a friendship. Still, there is definitely a core group of people at SP who seem to be very involved in each others' lives, and it's sometimes hard to see that and know that I'm not part of that. I do feel like I connect better with some of the non-moms at SP. I think it's because I deal with motherhood on a daily basis, and I just don't like spending my free time talking about children and motherhood. Of course it could also be that it's just too much effort for me to leave the house by 10 for a morning play date.

2/21/03

It's one thing to pursue spiritually based relationships with people you like, people who agree with your ideas and your beliefs. It's a whole other thing to commit to a relationship with someone who thinks differently. Both Jimmy and Daniel admit that they have completely different ideas about theology, about politics, about all the hot buttons in a relationship, but as Jimmy said, "Iron sharpens iron." My hope is that we can continue to show them our love and concern and that they will feel welcome in our lives even when we disagree. We could just avoid those issues, but what's the point? If we want to commit to each other, that means accepting and being open about the differences. One of the issues I'm dealing with is my tendency to forge relationships without allowing myself to go to that deeper level with people. Those fundamental differences are scary to me, and

From: Dave Ryding

For the past year I have seen God facedown on my knees. I don't know what God looks like from the past year, but I do know how he feels. I felt him next to me when I was alone and when I felt like I couldn't go on with everything. It felt like a comforting hand on my shoulder, a gentle push in the right direction and just the feeling I wasn't alone. If I didn't know any better I would say God looks like my buddies I see every week, but also has a strong resemblance to some friends I haven't seen in years.

----Original Message Follows----

From: Laura Bates

Being the outdoors person that I am, I can say that I most often see God's face when I look at creation. I know that it can be amazing to see God in the expansive, dramatic scenes of the mountains and the canyons, but for me, I see and hear God more intensely in places like wide-open prairie fields or in the shade of a forest. I think it is because those are the times when I am forced to be quiet and just listen to whispers.

----Original Message Follows----

From: Naomi Schwenke

About two years ago I was at a really confusing place regarding a relationship. I was fighting with God and trying to negotiate an outcome that wouldn't be painful for me. Finally, one night I literally crashed on my bed with a tearful stream of emotions. There was so much weight and pain on my shoulders, and I just couldn't take it anymore. I remember saying out loud to God, "I know what the answer is, but that's too painful for me to accept. I just can't." It's not every time one gets a response back right away, but this time I did. I heard the words as clear as day, "Yeah, but you're going to be okay." It was so powerful and still is today.

----Original Message Follows----

From: Bobbi Peacock

Grieving over the death of a close friend and my husband asking for a divorce within a week of one another...the reality that I was going to be a single mom, going back to work to support myself and Ella, living with the pain, the guilt, the shame. Moving cross country. Finding a job. Finding a place to live. Finding day care. Letting go of my daughter so that another woman may care for her. Broken heart. Broken dreams. I prayed and prayed and prayed. Night and day. Silently. Out loud.

The Lord was beside me, giving me STRENGTH and giving me hope. I FELT God.

I returned to Minnesota–bumped into Matt Henry, and he, at my inquiring, of course, told me about Solomon's Porch. I went to the first service on Christmas Eve alone, needing it to be everything I was looking for and praying for. Again I FELT the Lord saying, "This is your home."

I work for the nicest, sweetest man who is understanding and supportive of my challenge of being a single mom. My job is challenging, rewarding, and fun. Ella is thriving. Her relationship w/her father is thriving. I have the love and support of my family and friends and the people of Solomon's Porch. Life is good. God is great.

I haven't told anyone at the Porch how instrumental they've been to me in recovering from my divorce and grief of my loss...but I am grateful for each and every one of you.

God bless you all!!! Thank you all for accepting me and being my friend.

Bobbi

These practices have created an attitude in our community where people believe they can and should learn from one another. As a pastor, it's such a blessing to not be seen as the "Bible Answer Man," but as a member of the community, one who happens to have training, gifts, and a degree in theology. Even with this training there is no way any one person can, or should, understand and apply the Bible to the lives of everyone else. If we value the full immersion of our lives in the story of God as it is revealed in the Bible and desire for that story to creep into every vestige of our lives, we need the perspectives of many people. If my life has been smooth sailing, I'm going to get something very different from the stories of faith and life in the Bible than those who have suffered greatly.

The dialogical approach means that the authority of teaching and explanation needs to be decentralized away from me as the pastor both in the "pulpit" and during the week. I really enjoy this different role in our community. Even though I have found that I enjoy preaching and teaching, and there are even people who tell me they actually like listening to me talk, it's so refreshing for me to be one

I'm often afraid that if someone disagrees with me about a theological issue, they won't like me anymore. By telling and showing Chris and Daniel that I am interested in their friendship just the same, I think my real hope is that they'll feel the same way about me.

of the voices impacting a person's faith, and not to have the burden of being the only voice. In reality, people usually feel that their pastor's opinions on certain topics are important, and they will seek them out and honor them. But the pastor's input is almost always only one of the perspectives to be considered. My role is an important one, but it is part of, not the center of, our community. This has been freeing for me as I move from the "as the pastor I cannot bring my community any further in faith than I am myself" attitude. There is no question that our community leads me as much as I lead them. Our recent reading of 1 Corinthians, especially chapters 2-4, has encouraged me to participate in the community as a partner in faith and not as the pacesetter. What a beautiful thing to be part of a community that leads, teaches, and takes one another to places we could never be on our own. All that through something as simple as conversation.

If I Tried

If I tried to reach You Lord
Through works, I'd surely fall,
And if I tried to stand alone,
I know I'd miss Your call.

Night falls down in pairless sheets,
And no one knows her shame,
In distant lands where demons speak,
In thunder through the rain.

But you call me to come home,
And I can't live on my own

Chorus:
For no one can stand
And no one can boast
The only way to see Your face,
Is through your Holy Ghost.

If our tongues of angels speak,
And prophecy we claim,
And if we fathom mystery,
Taking credit for Your name.

Still You call us to come home,
And we can't live on our own.

CHAPTER 06

SPIRITUAL FORMATION THROUGH HOSPITALITY

WEDNESDAY

It's April 23, the Wednesday after Easter, and Shelley and I are hosting the weekly community dinner at our house. The Wednesday-night meal, which involves nearly every element of our life as a community, is one of the highlights of my week. This is when I often see us blessing each other's lives in tangible, meaningful ways. It's more like a family gathering than a church supper. There is no agenda, no meeting, no ulterior motive but to be together and open our lives to each other over a meal.

On Sunday night we announce the location and invite the entire community to eat together, so we never know how many people will show up; it could be 10, it could be 60. Tonight there will be something like 50 people arriving for dinner, including 17 children.

The SP folks tend to be last-minute kind of people, so our phone has been ringing all afternoon as people call to find out what they can bring for the meal. This is more than the strong Midwestern sense of needing to contribute. People like to feel they are part of the meal—not just showing up but actually joining in as cohosts for the night.

People begin arriving around 5 p.m., even though the meal doesn't start until 6:30. We're not quite ready for people to be here, but we're glad to have the help.

Tonight Shelley is preparing enchiladas: regular and a vegan version. With several vegetarians and others with special diets in our community, it's fairly common to provide different meal options for the Wednesday-night dinners and other community meals. Making more than one entrée sends the message that everyone is welcome, everyone belongs.

DUSTIN

Sunday, March 10

After a wild and crazy night at the mall, I drag myself out of bed around 10:30. This morning there is a brunch at Shana's house in south Minneapolis. It's become this routine, where every couple of weeks someone will volunteer their digs for morning grub. It's very similar to the Wednesday night dinners, but the clientele is more single, twentysomething, and bitter. Food ranges from Dustin and Eric's eggs and toast to Shana's fancy Shanacakes. As long as there is coffee, no one leaves unsatisfied.

I have no hope of ever hosting a Wednesday-night dinner at my tiny 600-square-foot studio, but maybe one of these days I'll motivate myself enough to fry up some hash browns and find my toaster.

By 6, the house is filling with conversation and the activities of setting up and meal preparation. We intentionally save a few jobs—setting the tables, tossing the salad, getting the plates out—until people arrive. These things are more easily done with help, and it's another way to let people know they are part of the "family" and they have something to contribute.

The result is a house hopping with people. Many just stand in the way in the kitchen, where people tend to congregate, but others are rummaging through our cupboards for glasses, moving tables around in the dining room, and cutting vegetables at the kitchen table.

The family room is crawling with young children; outside the older kids are playing on the trampoline. Children are an integral part of our community, and these meals are no exception. On this night, our daughter, Michon, is playing with Mindy's four daughters and our three sons are on the trampoline with Josiah, Emily, Isaac, and Lydia. Our children love anticipating who's going to be here tonight, and the parents of these children get the chance to pitch in, serve, and be served by others without having to focus solely on their children.

The house is starting to get warm, and it smells wonderful.

About 6:15, we hit a hitch. Kathryn didn't know our oven controls, so the enchiladas haven't been cooking. Actually, it's not a big deal. We normally eat at 6:30, rotating the inevitable latecomers into the dining room as others finish their meals. Well, tonight, we'll all eat at 7. It'll be a little more crowded with everyone crammed into our too-small dining room, but we'll manage. Some kids will head to the kitchen table or the basement, and others will eat on their feet in the kitchen, and we'll squeeze the rest into a place at a table so that we can all be together.

When the meal is ready, we invite those joining us for the first time to sit at the main table where we put our finest silverware and plates. We do this to honor them as our special guests and to give them the chance to meet the most people. Shelley asks a blessing on all who are in our home, and we eat.

I look at all these people sharing stories, laughing, passing the salad, serving each other, and I see a beautiful act of mutual hospitality.

As dinner ends, desserts are offered and dishes are cleared. Shelley and I don't have to orchestrate anything; people simply see what needs to be done and do it. A few people are washing dishes, breaking down the folding tables, moving chairs and table leaves, and putting things back where they belong.

Others settle on the couch to talk or gather in the kitchen to pick over the crumbs of dessert. As hard as it is to drag our kids away, Shelley and I take all four of them upstairs to get them settled for our bedtime ritual. It's clear that this meal is not just something we host, but that people are hosting each other in our house.

By 10:30 the house is free of guests, and Shelley and I head to bed. Lying there, I reflect on how I can pastor people who eat, serve, and clean in my home, people in whose homes I will eat, serve, and clean on another Wednesday night. What joy to open not just our church and faith to others, but also our home, refrigerator, cupboards, and closets. I don't feel I must wield authority over these people or keep some kind of professional boundary with them. It feels really good. This is the kind of life I once dreamed of.

Then, as is typical of my obsessive personality, the worry kicks in. I think about the people not here who normally would have been—is anything wrong? I replay the interactions of the night—what about those who didn't seem to engage with anyone? What about those who might feel lonely and isolated even on this night? What else can I do to get people feeling as connected as I do in our community? Then I think ahead to next week's dinner at Ben and Jen's—will we take that "magical step forward" into the kind of life I envision us living? Finally, I concede that it may not happen, and I decide to quit thinking about it. I fall asleep glad that there is a next week when we will gather together and serve one another again.

...

OPEN HANDS

We eat together a lot in addition to the Wednesday meals—a men's breakfast each Tuesday morning with no agenda beyond crowding into a small Cuban restaurant together, a monthly meal before our Sunday worship gathering, a huge breakfast hosted in a home after our Easter sunrise service, a regular habit of eating at a burrito place each Sunday that often feels more like church than many official church services I have been part of. People of our community have many impromptu meals with one another. There's always food available at our gatherings—at least a cup of tea or a peanut butter sandwich—and we keep a refrigerator at the church stocked so that anyone working there can get a snack. What's more, our members often bring meals to the gatherings to send home with families that need extra help for one reason or another.

Weekend events are discussed and next week's schedules dismantled. Everyone gets a chance to chime in, and everyone feels welcome. The gathering isn't formal. "God talk" or the church usually don't even become the center of conversation. It's part of the reason I like community. Real people are a part of it. That may seem simple, but I think it's really hard to achieve. All too often I've been part of church groups that don't allow themselves to be real people. It's like if they talk about frustration or grief or pain, that it's saying something about their walk. Other church groups I sampled had people that I'm pretty sure had never been outside their church walls. They hadn't been to a bar, or they didn't believe in going to movies. I couldn't hold a con-

versation that always was about God. Friday-night hangouts with churchy crowds always ended up with a discussion on urban ministry. So, anyway, full circle around, the Porch group is really committed to building relationships. Real people with real issues. God and our walk often come up, but it never seems forced or awkward. I just like that. And the Shanacakes soaked in maple syrup.

EASTER

We drug ourselves to the sunrise service and over to breakfast. It's all really hazy. Until I had my first cup of coffee around 8, my brain was on autopilot and not on record. I introduced my folks to everyone, and they took to simple conversations. "Why is Dustin so messed up? You two look normal, what happened? Why is Dustin eating that

Something special happens when we eat together, and to me it feels like what Jesus did. It is amazing how often in the Gospels Jesus eats and invites others to eat—there he is eating with sinners, eating the body and blood, eating after the resurrection to prove he was risen, and, in the book of Revelation, inviting the church to open the door so he can come in and eat with them. I am not suggesting an entire theology of eating together, but it seems to me that we cannot just pass it off as unimportant.

Here in Minnesota hospitality is often synonymous with food, but we work to ensure that our hospitality is not limited to meals. It's really about involvement in each other's lives and the act of welcoming the stranger. The real point of this brand of hospitality is the spiritual formation that takes place when we share the rhythm of regular life with one another.

Dinners hosted in homes let us practice our Kingdom living. As we join in the common rituals of stirring soup, washing plates, or folding tablecloths, we are entering into the most basic places of life. Sitting and eating in someone's house brings us closer to our true selves and to the place where spiritual formation accelerates.

At the same time, hospitality is about welcoming the outsider, the needy, and those from whom we are disconnected. Communal meals force people to eat with those they may not care for. It can be hard to live in reconciled relationships with each other—our insecurities, sin, and selfishness get in the way. When you see someone you don't care for at the mall, you can look the other way or duck into a store; at church you can focus on the "religious" activity or simply avoid eye contact. But regular acts of hospitality demand that we take stock of how we're doing. The intimacy of eating a meal together puts unreconciled relationships in a different context. You can't pass the salad dressing without looking at the other person. You can't ignore the other as you squeeze past on your way to your chair or hand over your dirty plate. It's hard to maintain the separated individualistic mentality of isolation when you're sharing a meal.

In an attempt to create the deeper connection I obsess about, there's a group that meets on Fridays. The group consists of somewhere around 20 people—married, single, with children and without. The group gathers most often at the Barnhills', but moves to other homes as well. Members have committed to making the meeting a schedule priority, being open and honest with one another, and being involved in one another's lives. They may or may not discuss books or study the Bible, but they will be there for each other, they will eat together, and they will live a committed life together. This group is extremely important to many who are part of it because it surrounds them with committed friendship. After nine months the group is clarifying its intentions and way of life together, but that evaluation can take place as they nurture and are nurtured by the promise of commitment.

CARLA

Thursday, January 30

Last night we hosted a Wednesday-night dinner. It was a good end to a day where I felt basically fried out from the time I woke up. By 4:30, I was praying Jimmy would come home early so I could grab a shower while the chicken for the enchiladas cooked. No luck. He walked in at 5:30, and I had to send him to the store for enchilada sauce. I finished making dinner at 6:15. Then Emily got a splinter in her foot, and we spent the next 15 minutes holding her while she screamed, cried, and convulsed on the bed. As I was lying on my daughter, who was screaming, "Dad, please stop!" I said to Jimmy, "I hope no one is in our living room right now." We finally gave up and walked out to the living room to find Colleen and Shana sitting on the couch. Thankfully, they didn't call Child Protection, and Emily showed them her splinter as proof that her screams were from the attempted splinter extraction.

Soon more friends join us—the Pagitts, Marlene, Colleen W., Eric (our red-headed friend). The kids head to the basement to eat, play, and watch a movie. We love having the Pagitts here, not just because we enjoy Doug and Shelly, but because their children love our children and vice-versa. Taylor dotes on both Emily and Isaac, and Chico and Ruben are so good about including both kids as they play here. It's like a night off for us. We can stay upstairs and participate in adult conversation.

Saturday, February 8

We had our Friday-night small group last night, which I think is becoming dull already. The last time we met, Jimmy suggested we read a book as a group, which I think is a good idea. When we first started, everyone shared the feeling that we wanted to be committed to each other and to building intimate friendships/community with one another. We didn't plan on doing a regular Bible study or anything formal. It seemed like we were all more interested in developing deeper relationships within the church. For the first several meetings, I think that was enough. But last night I felt like we really do need something to push us toward deeper conversations—they simply don't happen naturally unless someone is in crisis and is willing to bring that to the group. It feels like we need some kind of common topic to keep all of our conversations from being about '80s music and movies. Those kinds of conversations have been a good starting point as we get to know each other, but we can't move toward intimacy if we let ourselves stay there.

At the same time, I can see that our group has been meaningful to several people, including me. When we come in on Sunday nights, I know that there will be at least three people who will be glad to see me, people I can talk to because we have some common experiences

candle?" They did as well as they could, but I couldn't really enjoy the crowd as much as a normal gathering. I was torn between social interaction and feeling like I was abandoning my folks. However, I would do it the same all over again. I wanted my folks to put faces to names and see what type of setting my "crazy church" was. We really did read the Bible and try to follow in His path. Having couches doesn't make us bad, and the fact that the pastor wore a Hawaiian shirt last week doesn't discount anything he preaches.

It was also great to see the hospitality the Porch gave to the new faces. Everyone was eager to chat or find an extra folding chair. Later mom recounted, "I understand why you like the place, everyone seems like family."

We crashed at home for a couple of hours after the breakfast, but not for long. We geared up and headed to Colleen's for the annual "Orphan Easter Dinner." Now because I was bringing my parents, I wasn't sure I'd be invited, but I promised to bring the big-ticket item, the ham. About 20 gathered and spent a good part of the afternoon eating ham, homemade cranberry and cherry sauce, fresh baked bread, and garlic mashed potatoes. We shared stories of this and that, and my folks warmed up to the younger crowd.

SARAH

I like going to the Wednesday-night dinners whenever I can. Unfortunately, because I work two jobs, there are often times that I spend my

now. I've really valued Rachel's friendship. She is very quiet, which always throws me—I always assume other people are quiet because they find me dull. But she opened up to me one Friday about some struggles in her life, and I felt like she was someone I could trust to hear about my depression. I swear, when people are willing to be vulnerable, it cuts through the crap so quickly. I don't know why we all think we have to have it together. I look at our group, and almost without exception, we are all dealing with some very difficult issues—infertility, marital problems, depression, loneliness, unemployment, divorce—but these are all things we've learned to keep hushed up. Or we'll talk about the issue in an almost clinical way, but not the emotional or spiritual side of it. It's funny that even though we all like the openness and acceptance we feel at SP, we are so enculturated to keep ourselves closed up, especially in church.

A SPACE THAT WELCOMES

Like the other forms of spiritual formation discussed in this book, hospitality permeates every aspect of our life as a community.

Hospitality helps us be gracious with our lives and our belongings and impels us to loosen our grip on things we have. For example, Solomon's Porch owns a van that's available for anyone who needs it. The process for deciding who gets to use the van or for how long isn't very sophisticated: If the van is available, we let whoever needs it use it for as long as needed. This isn't a program for helping the poor; it's more like treating people as members of a family. If someone has a need we can meet, we will.

Hospitality also determines how we've structured and equipped our worship space. We take seriously the equality of everyone in the community, so it was an act of hospitality to decentralize the positions of power normally present in a church. For example, our meeting space for our Sunday worship gatherings is set up in the round and all on one level. There is no stage and no "front." People may go anywhere in the building; every room, including the office, is unlocked and accessible. In our gathering space it's generally possible to hear someone speak from nearly any part of the room without amplification, but hearing is hard when the room is full of people. We didn't want to resort to handheld or stand-mounted microphones that create distance between speaker and hearer. Instead, we hung six wide-range microphones from the ceiling to pick up speech from every part of the room. Thus everyone has the same opportunity to be heard as do the "official presenters." This we did as an act of welcoming and sharing, to show that everyone is free to share with the group and be heard.

Perhaps the most obvious expression of home-like hospitality in our worship space is our furniture. It only looks like coffeehouse cool—the real purpose of the used couches and end tables and armchairs is to make the room feel like home. (It didn't hurt that when we started out with no money for furniture these pieces came cheap.)

Over time it's occurred to me that our used regular household furniture epitomizes who we are seeking to be as a community. When we first began to receive used furniture and garage sale items, we talked about the fact that all of these pieces have a story. These used couches and chairs once had been chosen to fit just right in someone's home, then they were cast off, and now again they have a useful purpose in the church. As a woman of Solomon's Porch once commented, "These couches are a metaphor for our lives and what God is doing with us." Our furniture isn't pretty. It doesn't match. Some of the pieces need repairs. But it invites us, as the broken, used people we are, nevertheless, to find a worthy place in a community of faith. Brokenness can cripple, but not when we allow others to come alongside us and help us become whole.

To help us enter one another's lives in deeper ways, we invite members of our community to share their stories on a regular basis—at meals, through e-mail, on Sunday nights. This invitation is another way in which spiritual formation happens through hospitality.

When I say we share our stories, I don't mean classic church testimonies—at least, not always. Often people talk about issues that remain difficult for them to deal with. Sometimes they talk about their work or a ministry they're involved in. No matter what, we're careful not to make a person's story part of some bigger agenda or try to use it in a particular way. Doing so would mean these stories cease to be an open invitation into someone's life and become little more than sales pitches.

When people share their stories, they invite others into their lives. They open part of themselves that cannot be entered without permission. Those who listen sense a welcome to delve into their own stories, to make themselves vulnerable, to trust others with their pain. When stories are shared, individual experiences become communal experiences. This is hospitality at its most profound.

Wednesday night serving strangers in a restaurant hoping to make them feel somewhat at home. This is what happened last night. I got scheduled to work at the restaurant where I moonlight, while other people from Solomon's Porch gathered together to share a meal with each other.

I have to admit I was jealous. Since my family lives in Miami, there are often times that I miss that familial feeling of people eating together and just "being." No pretense, no one to impress, because we all have the same history and blood in our veins. Sure there are issues to be dealt with, just like when any group of people gets together, because who are we kidding? This isn't Utopia, but these people are the closest to family that Sarah and I have here in Minneapolis, and we love them.

I think the part that I like the best about the dinners is that everyone is invited to them. It doesn't matter if you have never gone to SP or if you have been there since its inception, everyone is welcome to be there.

That is a big issue for me, because growing up there were times when I was the one excluded from things, and I have made it into a sort of "mission" that other people don't have to feel disposable.

Wednesday nights are good because people are invited to be a part, and I like that.

2.18.2003
This morning I went to the men's breakfast at Victor's Café. It was blah. Maybe I was expecting more than just everyone

ERIN

Sunday, February 16

The annual church meeting today was productive and upbeat. I was particularly pleased at the way things were handled after such a negative service last Sunday. Our small prayer group addressed this dissension, but it was never directly addressed by Doug. During the meeting, about 8 others and I were accepted to the body as voting participants, and I felt I was entering a body that was unified and strong. We focused not on the turmoil within the church, but on all the new projects that required our ideas, participation, and prayers. Many new projects are things for which I have heart, including more extensive prayer, a tutoring/Bible study program for neighborhood kids, and music lessons at the church. I am excited to get more involved. I have been very involved in other churches, but none that I've felt so strongly about. Another new aspect of my church experience will be having prayer partners. These groups are formed with the intention of keeping each other accountable, and forming fellowship. I feel great about my prayer partners, Laura T. and Katherine K., around whom I feel comfortable and to whom I feel connected.

Tuesday, February 18

Throughout the weekend, I realized how much my longing for community stems from my family, and how blessed I am to have them as examples. My mother has 10 sisters and 2 brothers, most of whom live in South Dakota. Along with my other 50 first cousins, I was raised by many family members. We relied and continue to rely upon each other for different things. I had several hours to talk with my aunt. We talked about our families, our callings, and a lot about abundance. She and her husband are very generous people, and we shared about the blessings we have received after giving, and about how important obedience is. It was wonderful to laugh and talk with them.

Saturday, March 15

This evening was the first Women's Event at Solomon's Porch. Contrary to what some men I know believe, we didn't just sit around and giggle and say, "We're girls!" It was a wonderful evening to bond with females of all ages and dialogue about things that are of interest to women. I loved spending time with such a group of women, whose willingness to help and warm temperament make them feel like family.

HOSPITALITY AS SINCERITY

In order for hospitality to form us, we have found it must be sincere. When someone enters your home, there is a mandated transparency. When you open your door and offer your chair, you are inviting another person into your life in ways that transcend mere acquaintance and cultural comfortability.

Now there are people for whom this kind of openness is frightening. They spend the day (maybe more) cleaning and cooking and fussing to make their home appear to be something it isn't. This kind of "Martha Stewart" hospitality is not what we're striving for. Instead, we are seeking the kind of hospitality that says, "You are welcome in my life; there is little I am trying to hide here." In a way, it is a homecoming.

But hospitality isn't just about the host. The beautiful twin of sincerity is invitation—asking the other into your life. When you invite someone into your home, you are saying that you accept and trust that person enough to reveal new parts of yourself. When someone visiting Solomon's Porch for the first time is invited to a Wednesday meal, they are being included in one of our most intimate celebrations. They are invited to become part of our community.

Hospitality that is seen only as having food together is no longer a means of spiritual formation but an end in itself. It's possible for someone to come to a Wednesday-night dinner or a Tuesday-morning breakfast for no other reason than to eat; it's possible for a person to miss out on the real ways lives are blending and changing over Shelley's strawberry salad or Michelle's wheat-free bread. But those who want their lives to be touched, I believe, find real spiritual growth through efforts of sincere, invitational openness and hospitality.

Thom, a member of our community who has been extremely helpful in my thinking through this book, recently attended a play. Thom's a big fan of live theater, so I asked him what he thought. He said, "I felt as if the actors were merely quoting the playwright instead of living out the words expressed by the character." His response echoes our desire to be hospitable people who live the dreams of God in the way of Jesus. We seek to do more than quote the lines of our Lord. We dream of being people who attempt to do as Jesus did, humbly, by inviting others into redeemed life with us.

THE RISK OF HOSPITALITY

Naturally, openhandedness entails risk. When one is hospitable, one is exposed, vulnerable, and open for misuse. During the last three years, our attempts at openness and invitation have not always met with gracious acceptance and excitement. At times people of our community, including my family, have opened our lives to others only to be hurt. At times others have extended hospitality to us, and we responded in ways that were hurtful to them. This kind of pain creates an impulse to pull away and protect pride and emotions. Yet it

sitting around just BS-ing. I sort of wanted some more intentional kind of thing. I was sort of expecting it. I don't really know what goes on at one of these men's breakfast things since this was my first time ever to go to one, and maybe I had a false assumption.

I will give it another chance, but if it is just another chance to get together, sleep might just win out in the end. Besides, I have never been much of a breakfast person. I much prefer meals later in the day.

is precisely this risk that makes hospitality a meaningful element of spiritual formation in the Christian life. In these times we find the call to live the invitational life of our crucified Savior both heart-wrenching and life-encouraging.

A sort of "patent leather" spiritual formation—a glossy, slick substitute for the real thing—involves little vulnerability or self-disclosure. It is easy to sit in a Sunday-school class and listen to someone talk about spirituality and belief without opening up to its implications. There is a certain ironic comfort to a life that looks the part on the outside while wilting away on the inside. But when a friend tells you about a deep struggle, and the natural response is to enter in to that person's life, whatever the risk—then we find ourselves being transformed into the people of grace and mercy opened for us in the Kingdom of God. At its core, hospitality is an act of faith. It is faith in God and faith in people. It is an open posture that views others not as threats, but as participants in the process of one another's redemption.

The Body, True and Holy

The body, truly holy,
Incarnate
As the Father has sent me,
I am sending you.
Forgive, forgive, forgive.

Devoted to: teaching,
And life together,
To the breaking of bread,
Praying for bread,
And to prayer, prayer, prayer

Wonders and miracles
By the hands of the apostles
Everyone stood in awe
Stood in awe.

Chorus:
All the believers living together
Everything in common
Selling all their possessions. Everything they had.
They gave without question
They gave.

And the Lord added to them
Those being saved.
And the Lord added to them
Those being saved.

Alleluia amen.
Alleluia amen.
Alleluia amen.
Alleluia amen.
(Chorus)

Forgive, pray, give

CHAPTER 07

SPIRITUAL FORMATION THROUGH BELIEF

THURSDAY

My name is Janelle Nelson. On Thursday nights I so look forward to our community Bible study. There is something about a small group of about 15 people who get together to orient themselves around living life in a Jesus-like way. Our church does this as a body in other settings, but on Thursday evenings it is a smaller, more intimate experience. As I come up the stairs at 7 p.m. I get excited, because I know that the same people will be there, and all for a common reason. A sense of trust and dependence has been built over our weeks of meeting together.

This is my second session of Bible study. The studies normally run for sessions of 10 to 13 weeks and even require homework. I appreciate the work we all do to prepare, and I appreciate the structure. I need that in my life.

For a long time I went to Bible study because I could learn so much from others, and I left it at that. Now I go expecting that I will learn and contribute. There is a constant giving and receiving I have felt in this group that is expressed in such unique and spiritual ways. Everyone is at a different level, yet we are all striving for the same thing...to learn more about life with God.

In the beginning I held back from sharing because I didn't want people to see that I had struggles. In most of my other Bible study experiences I was the one leading, with my peers or with high school kids. Being open and vulnerable was hard for me. But it gets easier as time goes by. The people in the group are so different in background and lifestyle, and yet each seems to care about what everyone says and shares. The acceptance and sharing has allowed me to open myself up to others.

ERIN

5 March 2003

*Ashes on the fore-
head are a good
reminder to me of
how separated I
am from God. I've
been thinking a lot
about* sin. *The
word for* sin *in the
Greek New
Testament comes
from an archery
verb that means to
"miss the mark." I
love that. The word
sin has taken on
such a grave mean-
ing. But taken liter-
ally, sin is that
which separates us
from God and
makes us mortal. It
seems like the
Catholics have this
right—Lent should
be the season to
spend extra time
acknowledging the
disparity between
where our arrows
are landing and
where they should
and trying to make
amends for that
(although Jesus is
truly the only one
who is able to
make amends for
our sin).*

*I have always
felt loved by
boundaries and*

I have appreciated the variety of study. We have used both preset topics and formats we made up. Topics have ranged from examining spiritual health to a survey of the Old Testament. Sometimes we look at historical artwork related to the topic to deepen our understanding. The format includes discussion, lecture, and small-group conversation.

A few times during the sessions we have dinner at Marc and Alicia's home. They are the "leaders" of the study, though in reality we all con-tribute to what happens. It is a special time of fellowship to eat together and then have Bible study in their living room. These meals take our church community into homes and help us see how other people live and what they are passionate about. It is just another aspect where we share life togeth-er in a more personal way than I have experienced anywhere else. It has stretched me at times, but has also molded me. The prayer time each week has also been very powerful and a priority during our time together.

Our time Thursday nights has helped me to find more of myself and has helped me to see how God is working in other people's lives. This study helps me to see in a more tangible way that God is working all the time and in all kinds of situations. The Bible study lets me connect with people from my church and learn more about others, myself, and God.

...

WHAT DO YOU KNOW?

We all have some beliefs of which we are quite certain—that the sun will come up in the east tomorrow, that vinegar will taste sour, that it's best to avoid poi-son ivy. We know why we believe these things and can often even point to a process through which we came to believe them. This "knowledge" seems some-how the most authoritative kind of belief, the kind used to build a case about wearing long pants on a hike.

For the last few centuries, the Western worldview has the assumed belief that leads to spiritual formation comes about in exactly the same way. People start out as empty vessels—so the model goes—that must be filled with information, which leads to knowledge, which leads to right belief. Thus knowledge is power: If we give people the information to do something, they will do it, and if we give them information, they will believe. This perspective pervades education, busi-ness, art, entertainment—and the church, which has adopted it for spiritual for-mation with such vehemence that it can be hard to imagine a church's people coming to belief in any other way.

But the belief that leads to spiritual formation is not simply knowledge: It is centered in the way we understand and live in the world. Most beliefs are based on the ways we experience life, on the things that happen to us. We hold our most important beliefs at such a core level that we can hardly imagine not believing those things or explaining how we came to such beliefs.

The concept that knowledge comes through information is foundationalism—in rough terms, learning as a construction project. Information is the foundation upon which our hopes, ideas, and experiences rest. The foundation, then, is critical to sustaining belief. New information that coheres with the old strengthens the foundation; in contrast, information that seems contrary, weakens the foundation. If too much weakening is allowed, the entire belief may collapse like a skyscraper when the first floor is demolished. Formal debate depends upon this notion: Show that a line or argument rests on a faulty premise, and you've shown that the entire line of argument is faulty.

I understand this way of thinking because I used to think this way, too. I assumed that people based their beliefs upon certain sets of information, and so to get them to believe differently, I simply needed to give them new information. And I was good at offering new information that demolished someone else's point in order to lead logically to right belief.

If only belief really were that simple. I could send out an annual e-mail to my church to explain all the stuff of faith, then go to Bermuda for the rest of the year while all that good information reshapes hearts and minds.

But information alone rarely suffices to create belief; it needs to partner with other aspects of how we understand and live in the world. So the practices we are developing at Solomon's Porch are built on the understanding that belief is formed when information finds a partner with people's hopes, experiences, ideas, and thoughts.

Now I don't mean to disparage the cognitive process nor to downplay the importance of thinking right. Nor am I interested in arguing about whether thinking is more important than feeling or less. That's an old, tired argument. Instead, I'm suggesting that in belief there is always a complicated interaction, like a well-executed, spontaneous, free-form tango between information and one of the belief partners.

This isn't a radical new perspective but rather one that makes sense with the way most people come to understand new ideas. When information comes to us, we send it through a complicated grid of criteria: "Does this match with what I

responsibilities, and reading this Scripture, about how disciplined and faithful God wants us to be makes me feel grateful to have these stories, even though they scare me. Lately I've been thinking that struggle is very good for me. We build muscle by tearing and ripping it, then letting it heal and become stronger, and I think we build spiritual muscle the same way. I rest in faith that all of my trials have been put before me to strengthen my faith in Jesus Christ.

11 April, 2003
I had an orientation visit with my new chiropractor this afternoon. I can't believe the things that I am learning from her already, before I am even treated. She spoke to us today about the body's power to heal itself, and that the chiropractor can help the body do so by

decompressing nerves that are damaged by subluxation. She truly believes, as do I, that the world can be changed, person by person, with healing. She believes herself to be a messenger of hope, and has previously practiced at no charge to patients, but currently employs a different method of payment. She lets her patients set their own price for adjustments, believing that unless the patient pays something, they will not have made an investment in their own healing, according to the principle of sowing and reaping. I am struggling to set the price of my adjustments - I have insurance that would cover treatment from many other chiropractors, which would allow me to be adjusted for a $15 copay, and I will soon have all the free adjustments that I

already know to be reliable? Does it fit with my experiences in the world? Does it connect with the way I would like things to be? Does it fit with what I believe to be possible?" Information waits in the mind like a rider waiting at a bus stop until it can catch a ride with hopes, experiences, thoughts, or ideas to the place of belief.

There are people who are quite certain of their belief that human beings have never landed on the moon. They contend that what's been seen on television over the last 35 years is a fabrication perpetrated by the U.S. government in order to deceive us. This strongly held and, in their opinion, supported belief is not about the facts—it's about the violation of what they believe to be possible in this world.

As I'm writing this, my daughter is in the kitchen. Michon is using a hand-held sewing machine for the first time, and she is getting frustrated. She keeps saying, "This machine sucks," as if the problem with the sewing is centered in the machine. I've been trying to keep myself focused on my writing, but feel the need to inform her (not to use that language) that her trouble is more likely caused by user error than poor design. If I said this, she'd need to take that input and run it through her grid: "Is Dad trustworthy to say this? Have I experienced other times when this has been the case? Do I want the problem to be in the machine or in me? Is there something I have not read in the instructions?"

The solution to her problem is not going to be found in gaining new information alone. In fact, her ability to take in new information will be determined by whether it can connect with something else in her. If my advice gets hooked up with a belief partner, she'll either try a new tack or roll her eyes at me—depending on the partner. (Belief partners apparently go through adolescence, too.)

Recognizing that belief is not dependent on information alone has changed how I see belief in my own spiritual formation and that of others. A few years ago I had a conversation with a girl who held beliefs about animal rights and abortion different from my own. As we talked, it became clear to me that attempting to counter her information with my information wouldn't be useful. Her beliefs (and mine) were not based on information but on her hopes and experiences. I began to realize that someone can take in new information and understand it perfectly well without changing beliefs. Until I said something that jelled with her hopes and experiences, I would play no part in her formation of belief. I discovered there was no need for me to attempt to deconstruct her foundational belief—she wasn't going to let me, and I really didn't feel a desire to.

Rather, it seemed right to enter her life as an invited guest, one she could trust to suggest she swap her hopes. After that conversation, I began to wonder what my role as a spiritual guide would look like if, instead of focusing on disseminating religious information, I served more as an interpreter and suggester of alternative dreams, desires, and possibilities. The more I considered this option, the more excited I became: People who can change our beliefs are people to whom we give authority to suggest alternatives to us. It's hard to get around the idea of belief as a relational process.

At Solomon's Porch our desire is to form friendships where we are invited into each other's lives with a level of trust that allows for spiritual formation. We can learn from one another because we have proven ourselves trustworthy.

Some people will be concerned that this view of knowledge is too relativistic, as though all ideas are open for reconsideration at the whims of those who are offered those ideas. But the truth is, that's really how belief works. We all have held beliefs that worked quite well in one setting but failed miserably when we tried to transplant them. This is often the case with students who enter college or adults who move to other countries. Sometimes it happens in the face of tragedy, where all that we thought we knew is thrown down. All that we learn after that point of reorientation will partner with the new situation—and, disconcerting as the experience is, our beliefs will change.

This malleability of our beliefs isn't bad. In fact, there is considerable good to the challenge of living a faith that's based on more than information and that is connected to the frailty of our humanity. In our community we've found that this understanding of belief actually helps us take risks by keeping us open to ideas we haven't had yet. It's a beautiful thing when, during our Bible discussion group, someone responds to an idea with, "I've never thought of it that way!" The sense that spiritual formation is happening in that moment is palpable. What's more, it's often traumatic to be forced to question something we're not ready to question—but when we accept that everything is questionable at one point or another, we are more ready to at least talk through those questions.

In our community, we've found that mingling information with hopes, experiences, ideas, and thoughts often brings with it wonderful surprises. Bringing information alongside belief partners creates a fascinating kind of mutuality as all of the partners shift and grow with the contributions of the others. My belief that God is loving will be affected when the hopes of an infertile couple are fulfilled in a pregnancy. That experience will affect the way I talk about God's love with someone else. That person's experiences will affect the way he responds to

could ever want as I enter chiropractic school. But I feel that God has brought me here to teach me things about being a good chiropractor—how to spread hope, and practice with abundance—that I won't learn in school. I feel strongly that I need to treat with her.

DUSTIN

8:40 a.m. That's my cut-off time for the bus. If I leave any later than that I will surely stand at the stop for 10 minutes. Leave anytime before 8:41, and I'm sure to not stand long. I think it has something to do with rush hour or something, but all I know is that if my microwave says 8:41, I best be bringing an extra scarf.

Every morning it's the same. It takes about 15 minutes to get to work, and every day is another magical adventure. Some days I get to watch the driver trade jokes with the elderly lady with bad hearing.

Sometimes I find a friend to sit next to and trade small talk with. "How's the job? Good. Yeah, crazy weather." Often I scout a newspaper to ease the dullness by a fraction.

Other times I get even luckier, and I get to watch the single moms try and manage their four kids or enjoy the scent of a homeless guy passed out in the back. I've heard one side of a break-up phone call and women discussing their test results. Hearing snippets of other people's lives always keeps mine in perspective. Sometimes I get lonely listening to a lovesick couple chatter on about their evening plans or new home. Other times I feel fortunate because I'm not the one

my words, and his response will affect the way I talk about God's love in the future. This process in no way devalues information, but elevates the partners of belief to an equal level of importance.

We are seeking to bring information alongside belief partners in a variety of ways. As with all of life in our community, these experiments shape us in ways we rarely expect.

LIFE DEVELOPMENT FORUMS

In 2002 we began offering our version of adult formation classes, which we call Life Development Forums. As is so often the case in the Bible, the things of the Kingdom life are the ordinary, everyday issues of earthly life. So in our Forums we have studied Spanish, read the Old Testament, done massage, explored our areas of strength, written or read poetry, and have looked at dating, photography, natural health, parenting, and budgeting. These forums let us share information, hopes, desires, ideas, and experiences for living our lives in good, healthy, productive ways.

JAVIER

1.30.2003

So last night Sarah and I went to see Jesus Christ Superstar. *I was disappointed. Not because the story isn't good or because the characters of Judas and Mary Magdalene weren't played well. It was Jesus' fault. Sebastian Bach (Skid Row front man) played Jesus. I knew this beforehand, but I wanted to give him the benefit of the doubt. His acting was just terrible, and his singing wasn't much better. I don't want to sound like an opera snob who critiques every nuance of a show. I am pretty easy to please when it comes to seeing artists perform, but I just was not impressed by their selection of Bach as Judas. It was the 3rd or 4th time that I had seen the show, so I did have a frame of reference.*

A couple of lyric lines did stand out to me though. Judas said/sang, "…but every word you say today/gets twisted round some other way…"

This got me thinking about how often we miss the message of Christ due to our biases and different contexts. Not that the original hearers of Christ weren't influenced by their biases or expectations (obviously). Then I wonder how we can really know the message of the gospel. I guess the role of the Holy Spirit is much more important than expected in our pursuit of the way of Jesus.

The other song that really affected me was called "I Don't Know How to Love Him." It is a song from the perspective of Mary Magdalene and her struggles of how to love this man (Jesus) who scares her. I wonder why there are so few Christians gutsy enough to write songs of such depth. I could name names and songs, but that wouldn't be very productive I don't think. I wonder though how true to the entire Christian story are the songs that focus on just the "Shiny Happy People" stuff. I guess we need some of that, but as with the things we eat, we need a balanced diet of different world views. Maybe the Christian music industry has caused a deficiency in our view of God and the way Christians interact in the world, which in my opinion includes a deep sense of mourning or loss.

Mourning over the fact that though this world can at times be an amazing place, it is still under the curse.

Sometimes I wonder if color or taste or touch would be any different in a world that was fully redeemed.

PROFESSIONS OF FAITH

We've found professions of faith to be a powerful way for people to learn about and participate in a confession of belief. Sometimes we use a well-known piece like the Apostles' Creed or a particular section from the Bible like the Doxology from Jude, or other times we use prayers from the rich history of Christianity.

I have to admit, this is new territory for me. I used to think that asking people to profess something they didn't yet believe was tantamount to making them lie. Why ask someone to say in a crowd what she is not comfortable saying on her own?

But I've come to see that the process of believing anything begins with trying it on. Some people cannot fully believe something without saying it out loud to see how it feels and sounds. It is as if believing follows the confession. When we invite people to confess a faith that is not yet fully theirs, we are inviting them to walk into faith and spend time there.

Similarly, I used to think that it was hypocritical for people to confess Christian belief out loud and then not live up to it. In most cases, however, people are in a state of becoming, not a state of hypocrisy. Their profession is not a lie; it is a longing—not a statement of how things are but a pleading for how they want things to be.

Confessions of faith invite people into situations where the information in their heads can connect with the desires of their hearts. When the content of the profession meets people's hopes and propels them toward a way they are not yet living, then these professions become spiritually forming.

getting evicted or sent off to treatment. It's a startling way to start the morning, and I try to remember to use the time to reflect on where in this mess of a bus I'm supposed to fit in.

Once I'm off the bus, I have a brief four-block jaunt to my office tower. On the way I pass a dance club that caters to bachelorette parties and 18-year-old girls, a piano teacher's studio, and the busiest abortion clinic in Minnesota. Man, the fun never stops.

Okay, to get it over with, I'm pro-life, but anti-government. I don't think the government should have control over what someone does, even if I have moral objections to the issue. But my opinion isn't the point or even all that interesting. I find it interesting to watch the ways people support their "Christian causes."

Every single day I've walked by the clinic I've seen at least one woman standing by the curb, handing out pamphlets and offering words of wisdom to prospective clients. The dozen or so regulars have a look. Late 30s, unkempt long brunette hair, usual-ly pulled back into a bun. Heavily used winter jackets from decades past, and a handmade scarf. It never matches their tattered mit-tens and often just makes their giant windshield glasses look even bigger. Pink and blue pho-tocopied pam-phlets, worn at the edges from being handled every day. Sometimes they will have rosary beads, and often I hear them singing hymns softly to themselves.

JIM

2/18/03

Tonight's meal with Emily and Isaac began with "Blessed be God, Father, Son and Holy Spirit... and blessed be His Name forevermore" as we crossed ourselves. Doing this with my kids just reminds me of this desperate need I have to continue to explore this tradition in the church (the liturgical one), and how hard it is at SP to do this. It's not really who we are, but there's space there to explore it. We discussed Christian practices like this for a few weeks, but how can I explore this part of the faith if it is not really who the community is? This is a very difficult thing for me to figure out.

3/02

It's 6:30 a.m., dark, and depressing as I head out the door to go to work. The kids are in bed, and I'd give a million dollars to be lying right beside them. This year has been the most difficult year of my life emotionally. The kids I work with are so aggressive. I've been kicked, hit, and scratched so many times that it has become normal. At lunch, I hide in the nurse's office to get away from the screams (not laughter, but screams of kids in crisis). Of course, I get called every name in the book, but that doesn't phase me a bit. It's when a student tries to hurt me or hurt someone else that I have to work so hard to stay in control. I see a light at the end of the tunnel. Two more months to go. One thing that is helping right now is to get out of the car at school and to say a short prayer, "May all the things that I do and say be to your honor and glory." That way, I figure that when/if I have to physically restrain a student, I can think on this and keep the anger at bay.

SERMON

At Solomon's Porch, sermons are not primarily about my extracting truth from the Bible to apply to people's lives. In many ways the sermon is less a lecture or motivational speech than it is an act of poetry—of putting words around people's experiences to allow them to find deeper connection to their lives. As we read through sections of the Bible and see how God has interacted with people in other times and places, we better sense God interacting with us. So our sermons are not lessons that precisely define belief so much as they are stories that welcome our hopes and ideas and participation.

This approach hasn't been without its challenges. In many ways we are seeking to redefine the pastor/parishioner "contract." Many people select churches by the pastor and the content. They want someone they already agree with, but who is just far enough "ahead" of them to help them grow. They believe the pastor is the sole (or at least primary) teacher and keeper of the things of God. Often this assumption is so firmly held that people feel no need to think for themselves or to think of themselves as participants in one another's redemption. They are content to let the pastor decide where they stand on issues and how they will discuss those issues with one another. Or they quietly disagree with the pastor and leave it that way.

This "contract" gets even more confusing when people select a church using many of the same criteria they use when they purchase a car, pick a movie, or select a therapist. There is tremendous pressure for a pastor to create a setting in which people feel that their time is well-spent, that they got something from the night, that they were "fed."

In a recent staff meeting we talked about the occasional person who doesn't feel "fed" at Solomon's Porch. We mused about the kinds of people who need to be fed—babies, people without use of their hands, people too weak to serve themselves. We concluded that "being fed" ought to be a strange metaphor for what happens at church but that it is sadly appropriate. For it seems that the church has trained Christians to expect someone to give them faith in small, prechewed bites they can swallow without significant effort.

To move beyond this passive approach to faith, we've tried to create a community that's more like a potluck: People eat and they also bring something for others. Our belief is built when all of us engage our hopes, dreams, ideas, and understandings with the story of God as it unfolds through history and through us.

This is not to imply that belief is a free-for-all—as pastor I certainly do not sit idly by and let people believe whatever they want—but I am by no means the only one seen as the teacher. We hear from multiple voices throughout the week, including Sundays, and welcome the ideas and inspirations of every person in our community. This is living life together, and it's not all about the transfer of information.

SARAH

3/3/03

On another topic completely, Javier and I were listening to a CD about Rich Mullins the other day. It had some radio interviews with him—he was a very bold man. Sometimes I can't believe the things that came out of his mouth. He commented on something I thought was really profound, and I've been thinking about it ever since. He said that he never wanted to be used by God; rather, he desired to be wanted by God. God can use anyone he wants—more

However, on occasion they bring their sandwich-board friends. The board guys proudly display pictures of aborted fetuses and chant religious catch phrases for all to hear. I've seen mothers scoop up their children and navigate across a busy street just to avoid walking by the grisly images. Kids not old enough to understand stop and ask questions.

In the two years I have walked by the clinic, I have developed a lot of respect for the homely women. I have seen people berate them, brush them off, or do the occasional, classy spit. Their humble demeanor offers a sense of respect for everyone involved. They have a strong conviction and are willing to brave the weather and do something they feel makes the world a better place. They must have a decent suc-

cess rate; otherwise I think they would have found a different tack by now.

However, I have a bone with the sandwich-board guys. Their radical scare tactics only frighten everyone and push moral views off into the "religious zealot" category. I fear onlookers walk by and hear the guys screaming at clinic workers and leave thinking, "If Christians think this is loving and compassionate, I want no part of their world."

often than not, they're not "good" people: Judas, Pilate, the man who physically nailed Christ to the cross... They were all people "necessary" to the gospel. The only "necessary" disciple was Judas—the other 11 were there because Christ wanted them to be. They didn't necessarily have a specific purpose. To be used... or to be wanted... it's a fascinating thought. Especially when the entire Christian world (and I suppose by this I mean the evangelical world I was brought up in) is constantly pushing you to discover God's plan for your life and how to let him "use" you.

4/8

Tonight Javier is meeting with some people about the upcoming Way of the Cross art event. Since they're in our living room, I have some time to kill shut up in the bedroom. I finally started reading The Myth of Certainty *by Daniel Taylor. I've wanted to read it for years—since the middle of college at least—but I've been too burnt out on "formal education" to attempt to read anything "intellectual" since then. The church book club read it together, and I even went to the breakfast at Deborah's house when we got to discuss it with Dan himself. I read the intro and about 5 pages tonight and had to stop so I could think about it for a while. I want so badly for this book to be a breath of fresh air for me. Perhaps that's why I've put off reading it for so long—I didn't want to be let down. My soul has been aching for years in a way that I can't describe, and I want this book to ease that discontent. I have my doubts. "One bright young woman expressed to me a whimsical desire for the simple, naïve view of life she once had as an active member of her church's high school youth group. But with a quiet earnestness she observed, 'I can't unlearn what I've learned since then" (pg 18). I really was happy then. I enjoyed being evangelical. My life made sense. Something has happened to me since then. I'm still not content. I'm thankful for S.P., though, because I wouldn't be going to church otherwise. I wasn't before that. "Because my mind sought answers ceaselessly to the important questions in life but at the same time rejected all answers to those questions, and almost even the possibility of answers. I was a prime candidate for misery and cynicism" (pg. 17-18). The first few pages have struck a strong chord.*

THE BIBLE AS AUTHORITATIVE COMMUNITY MEMBER

Through the centuries the church's relationship with the Bible has been described in various ways. Some traditions show submission by carrying the Bible into worship over people's heads. Others speak of the Bible as the foundation on which they stand. Still others view it as a clue book to the faith of the past.

In addition to these helpful postures, we refer to the Bible as a member of our community of faith–an essential member that must be listened to on all matters on which it speaks. This approach is meant to strengthen rather than diminish the Bible's authority. When we read the Bible in our community, we attempt to fully engage ourselves in it and in the God who inspired its creation. We work to listen to the community of faith that has produced us and the God who dwells in us. We focus our efforts on trying to figure out if our lives could be relevant to the story of God, not if the Bible can be relevant to our lives. We can only do this when we allow the information gleaned from the stories of the Bible to couple with our experiences, hopes, and ideas.

The Bible can be difficult to understand, sometimes because of cultural differences between the ancient world and ours, and sometimes because of phrasings or approaches that simply seem to violate our 21st-century sensibilities. In our community this difficulty seems to happen on a regular basis. Perhaps it's that we are inquisitive, or perhaps we look at a large section at a time and therefore can't avoid some truly puzzling or contradictory parts of the Bible. Whatever the reason, we seem to run into "I'm not sure I like what this says" moments fairly often.

Yet we try to treat the Bible as the sort of best friend to whom one gives the benefit of the doubt. At some point you have to shrug your shoulders and say, "I don't know what she means, but I'm sure she meant well." Parts of the Bible may seem unpalatable or incomprehensible in our time, but that doesn't entitle us to step away from the Bible, ignore it, or even try to reduce the complexity to simple teaching principles. Rather, because the Bible is part of our community, we are called to step toward it and see what it has to offer us in areas of hopes, experiences, thoughts, ideas, and information. We need to allow the Bible to share with us those things that correct us, teach us, and lead us, even when we don't understand or like what it says. Seeing the Bible as a crucial part of our community is a relational commitment that extends beyond any intellectual commitments we will form.

At bottom, our trust in the Bible does not depend on information that "proves" the Bible to be credible. We believe the Bible because our hopes, ideas, experiences, and community of faith allow and require us to believe.

The understanding of belief I've outlined leads beyond traditional education-based learning in ways that can take people out of their comfort zone. People are complex beings with tangled histories, and it's naïve to expect that a single comprehensive system of learning can lead all of us to exactly the same conclusions. At Solomon's Porch we want to live out the conviction that ideas, hopes, experiences, and understandings play essential roles in the life of our community, and we continue to spur each other on to be spiritually formed by our beliefs.

Hungry People

So they pulled out loaves and fishes
And these they got from a little boy
With nothing more than a basketful of wishes
That would have barely fed the kid

You were there to feed a hungry people
To show you give us daily bread
And as the bread was broken did you wince?
Knowing your hour would be ahead?

The sand was hot beneath your feet
And you didn't eat for forty days
When you were weak, Satan came to tempt you
Saying, "Dare you to turn this stone to bread!"

You came to feed a hungry people
So we don't live on bread alone
I know you're God, but do you ever wonder
Why we ease our hunger eating stone?

If we asked you to teach us, Rabbi
How to speak and touch your heart
You would know above all others
How to finish what we can't start

You came to feed a hungry people
To give us life through our daily bread
Through the fruit of the blood you shed
We find life abundant once again.

CHAPTER 08

SPIRITUAL FORMATION THROUGH CREATIVITY

FRIDAY

It's 7:56 p.m. on Friday night. Despite our efforts to appear organized and competent, we're still running a half hour behind schedule.

I'm Thom Olson. Together with Javier Sampedro and Luke Hillestad, I'm coordinating (read: herding) over 30 painters, sculptors, musicians, actors, and dancers within our community in "The Way of the Cross." This is our version of the 14 Stations of the Cross to commemorate Holy Week.

Each of the Stations is being presented with a visual element and a performance element. People are supposed to walk through an "art gallery" along one wall of our gathering space and view the visual compositions in order, then sit down to watch as the same stations are depicted through music, drama, dance, and film. This way each person gets more than one opportunity to enter into the story.

Or at least they would, if we could ever get this performance started. We had thought the gallery walk would be done and the performances well underway by now because a certain pastor (who will remain anonymous but answers to "Hey, Doug") had told us to plan for "oh, 75 people or so." But a quick head count confirms that over 200 people are still waiting in the lobby downstairs! It's like a rush-hour traffic jam on I-94, thanks to our quaint insistence on ushering people up in groups of seven or eight.

Time to formulate Plan B.

I talk with Luke and Jav, and we decide to give it a couple more minutes. "Minnesota nice" strongly influences behavior around here: To start with so many people still in the lobby would be rude. We remind ourselves that having couches means people can at least sit in comfort while they wait for us to get our act together.

In spite of how things look, tonight is the culmination of several months of dreaming, planning, and collaborating.

ERIN

20-22 February, 2003

In the evening, I went to church, where I had my first guitar lesson with Luke. His teaching style will be a great match for me—combining theory and functional technique. In the past, I've had 30-minute lessons on how to hold a guitar pick, so to have learned as much as I did during the first lesson felt wonderful. I feel so glad to have a teacher so that I will need to be accountable and practice more. Luke and I talked about how strange it is to exchange money as a community. I feel great about supporting artists and healers, so they can continue to grace and bless the lives of everyone else.

Saturdays are usually my favorite days. Today I taught 13 piano lessons, mostly in one neighborhood. I really enjoy work-

Those of us involved in the event met regularly after the Sunday-night gatherings for anywhere from 20 minutes to an hour and a half. Each week we'd ask, "Anyone got anything they'd like to share or try out?" Invariably, somebody would test out a sample lyric or get feedback on a new chord progression, show off a half-finished painting or recite a few paragraphs from a not-quite-memorized monologue. Now that's something you don't see every day: artists willing to be vulnerable and risk looking unsophisticated as they share their half-baked ideas.

Part of what made the process memorable was the generous cross-pollination among the artistic disciplines—painters offered honest feedback on a dramatic monologue, actors reflected on what moved them in a piece of music, and musicians suggested new ways to clarify and enhance a visual composition. The art we created with each other became an honest expression of our communal ethic: What we do together is far better and more important than what any one of us can do alone.

I'm aware that some pieces have been totally reworked since our final meeting. Come to think of it, we never really did rehearse the moment when Jesus dies on the cross—the Christ Candle gets snuffed out, and the room is supposed to go pitch black. Shoot, there are a lot of candles in this room...should have probably thought of that beforehand. Will it work if we blow out three candles after each station's performance? I don't know. I decide to see what Jav and Luke think.

I catch Luke giving me a look. We've waited long enough—it's time to dim the lights. I guess we'll have to figure this out as we go along...

HOW I GOT INTO THIS

I have long lived with a real admiration of creative people. I am particularly attracted to people who can imagine what could be and live to bring that vision to fruition. Now my awe may be due to my almost complete lack of artistic ability—I swear I have either a music learning disability or avant-garde harmonizing capabilities that most people simply have not caught up to yet. Regardless, I am intrigued by those who see the world in ways that others do not.

It's probably no coincidence that my first brush with Christianity came in the form of a play I attended in high school—a passion play. Even as I realized that "passion" didn't mean what I had thought, I could feel my heart being opened in new ways. I found myself drawn into the story, to the intensity of the experience, to the sheer magnitude of the drama. By the end I had a strong sense that something here was to have my life. It felt natural to follow the instructions of the person on the stage and join others backstage to talk with some "caring people." I hoped one of these strangers could help me understand the pull in this story that I couldn't put my finger on.

Once I got backstage, however, the mood changed from emotion to instruction. As I recall, someone read through a little booklet that explained the truth behind what I'd just seen. I listened and learned and decided to give my life to this call. The majority of my mentorship in Christianity from that point on came from people who, like me, reasoned their way through life. Still, as my intellectual faith training proceeded, a hidden and even dormant part of me saw artists as mysterious, almost otherworldly.

That dormant part woke up when I started going through my great awakening and seeking after things I knew nothing about. I was almost sure there was something of God I needed that I could not even see, something that had to come from this place of creation, of vision, not knowledge or intellect. I wondered if a deeper life with God might be found in the hidden corners of artists' rooms.

A staleness was growing in me that I knew I couldn't purge on my own. I didn't need someone to say "think outside the box." I could think perfectly well. I wanted to be led to places where thinking was not the sum of spiritual life, where thinking could be joined with experience, emotion, and imagination. I hoped that artists could show me the secret places of faith in which to find God.

When we were conceiving Solomon's Porch, we didn't set out to start a ministry to creative types. I did not presume myself to be one who could reach artists. Rather, I hoped they would reach me, that they would show me those secret places of faith I had only imagined. I hoped I would find God there.

We attempted to find ways for creativity to be sewn into the fabric of our community, not as an add-on, but as a fundamental part of our spiritual formation. The hope was that we would be a community where, as one of our dreams puts it, "Beauty, art, and creativity are valued, used, and understood as coming from the Creator." Again, this was not an attempt to market the church to artists, but an invitation for them to lead our community.

In so many ways, that's what's happened. As Solomon's Porch has grown, we have become a community of artists—both professionals and dabblers. Their presence in our community has opened us up to a way of life that allows for spiritual formation through creativity.

ing with children one on one. Learning about their personalities and how they work best is the most interesting challenge for me. Teaching really has increased my patience as well. Most of the families for whom I work know that I am a believer, and they are Christians as well, so I feel free to talk about beauty (in music and other arts) and how it relates to God.

My lesson went well. It set the stage for Friday evening, when my best friend Sue came to visit. We had a nice dinner, and stopped by the art lounge at the Porch. The photography and music were amazing. I love being in a place where there are people who inspire me and intrigue me and stretch me to be a better musician than I am. After the lounge we skipped out on an '80s party in favor of going home to play some music. I was so glad we did because we had a songwriting experience that could only be considered a gift. We had lyrics, a melody, a guitar and a piano part in a matter of minutes, and deem it our best song yet. I wish Sue lived here in Minneapolis so we could play together more. Things just flow so easily when the two of us work together.

5-28-03
The presence of women in music at Solomon's Porch is noticeably absent, or weak at best. In the year that I have been going to church at the Porch, I have only heard two women perform, as opposed to about a dozen men. What is harder yet for me to swallow is that the majority of our church songs, as beautiful and well-written as they

To be honest, I had real doubts about how to make artists a vital part of our Christian community—not theological doubts, but experiential. Art and artists are used to support the agenda of more than one church, but I'd seen few if any churches that welcomed artists as leaders on a par with the thinkers and preachers. The church where I worked for 10 years was not short on people, we had 17 softball teams for crying out loud, so clearly there was no shortage of people—but both the youth ministry and the church as a whole often had to hire musicians. Drama people were available—but it seemed that they were called on mainly to illustrate the spoken sermon, to break up the routine for a week, or to do the occasional dinner theater show. A few pictures graced the walls—but otherwise artists were almost as hard to find as fill-in nursery workers.

What struck me is not that these people and their attendant gifts weren't there, but that nobody noticed their absence. The church's life and spiritual formation were perceived as complete without them. I must say our ministry was wonderful even without a deep connection with artists. So my fear for Solomon's Porch was that we would fall into the same way of thinking. Without a model for how to make creativity a part of our lives, I wasn't sure we should or could pull it off.

As it turns out, I underestimated what can happen when creative people are given permission to give life to their dreams. Admittedly, we were in a position of starting with something new, rather than trying to apply new ways of thinking to old models. That allowed us to imbed creativity into our life as a community from the beginning.

It helped that we approached the prospect of living as a creative community with a combination of openness and productive cynicism. There can be a tendency in Christian circles, especially ones that venture into new territory, to complain about how things are. But creativity is providing a new way of living, seeing, hearing, or being, and we were blessed with several people who love the process of seeing a possibility and turning it into something tangible. So we allowed ourselves to look at something with cynical eyes only if we were committed to working on it. We agreed not to gripe about contemporary worship music without undertaking to create music that moved us away from those concerns and into a new way of understanding. We agreed not to whine about the lack of art in churches without determining how and why art would play a role in our community.

Since that time, we have become a community of creative people—not just artists, but people who are full of ideas about how life can be and how we can bring blessings into the world. We have teachers and designers and writers and therapists and yoga instructors and musicians and dancers and actors and more—all kinds of people who are committed to exploring new ways of thinking, of expressing, of living. Together we are working to create a life that we hope is truly beautiful to God.

When churches think through who they are and who they want to be, they face a choice: Do they create programs for the people who are there or for the people they want to attract? We tried to avoid that choice altogether. Instead we asked who we were and what we had to offer one another. We weren't out to make Solomon's Porch a church for artists, but it has evolved as an attractive home for creative people. In being faithful to the call of creativity we've seen Solomon's Porch become a place where imagination, hope, and faith find the room to get to know each other. And what they create together can be breathtaking.

JIM

4/17

I don't know what to say. I've longed to worship God in a way in which I felt I could show deep reverence and awe, while also enveloping myself in God's presence and mystery; tonight, I got the chance to do that very thing at SP. We also got the chance to show others, as best we could, the beauty of worshiping God using forms of worship that come from Catholic and other "high church" traditions. Carla and I put together a worship service that celebrated the last supper of Jesus and his disciples, followed by a march of the whole congregation to an altar where we placed the cup and bread of communion, the cross, the Christ candle, and Holy Scripture. Overnight, members of SP came to the altar and kept a vigil at the altar as a way of reenacting the agony of Christ in the garden of Gethsemane. We tried to create a solemn atmosphere, one in which everyone could reflect both on the tragedy awaiting Jesus on his last night and also the stunning message he left his disciples with. (That we had the explicit blessing from Doug to organize this service, without any need on his part to oversee things, is no small thing. It isn't lip service when it is said that "Your dreams can become the dreams of others at SP." Never did we hear, "But we don't do things that way here.")

At 6 a.m., Janelle, Dan, and I were ending the Vigil. The light was coming up, and it reminded me that it was at this time that Christ was beginning to be crucified. The three of us ate the remaining bread and wine, leaving the cup and plate empty. Then the connection between the empty altar and the crucified Jesus struck me. This visual reminder of the despair brought to Jesus and his disciples in the crucifixion was the last of many experience's of God's grace I had during this whole evening. Thank you, God, for meeting me in this experience.

---

are, are not in a singable range for females at all. I've heard some females harmonize to the songs, but a lot of women choose not to sing along at all or sing uncomfortably. I would love for women to take more ownership in music at church, especially since talent oozes from the women at the Porch. In general, I'm a person who likes to fill any need that I see, but this one is difficult for me. I have contrary needs—to express myself, and to be private. So as a musician with a lot of training but terrible performance anxiety, I certainly don't feel comfortable trying to bridge this gap by myself. I have been talking about collaborating with some women— writing some songs, performing in small groups. This prospect is very exciting to me.

SPIRITUAL FORMATION THROUGH CREATIVITY

Our efforts at living lives of creativity certainly make our community a more beautiful and interesting place to be. Our space is filled with art—paintings, sculpture, photography. When we moved, the artists took over the painting of the worship space so that we now gather in a room painted a mellow shade of purple with accents of green and orange and gold. Nearly every Sunday something changes—a swag of fabric is added to frame the screens we use to display lyrics and Bible passages, a more interesting table is set near the center of the room, a candle has been moved into the prayer room to create a more serene vibe. Aesthetics—and all that it stirs in us—matters to our community.

But this desire to be people who live creatively and for whom creativity is a kind of spiritual formation goes far beyond hanging lovely drawings on the walls or filling our couches with lots of people in funky shoes. Instead our creativity comes from a desire to live life as people who are created in the image of a creative God, who are invited to be co-(re)creators with God.

In recent decades, the story of God has been understood in terms of creation, fall, redemption, and exit from this world. This view implies that God's relationship with the world sort of cooled off after the fall and didn't really jump back in until Jesus came along. Apart from the problems created by basically discounting everything between Genesis 3 and the New Testament, this idea marginalizes our human activity in the world. It puts humanity in a passive role in which things simply happen to us—we are created, we are afflicted by sin, we are redeemed, we are brought to another place—and all that's left to humans is to find creative ways to sin.

A different way to understand the story goes more like this: God, the creator of all things, has been re-creating all things through the redeeming work of Jesus the Messiah. In this view we are not left with a memory of a God who made this world and now simply waits for it to expire. God is constantly creating anew. And God also invites us to be re-created and to join the work of God as co-(re)creators. We are not bystanders, nor are we to be inactive.

The gospel is packed with the implication that we have something to give because of our redemption. We are told to go, to make, to build, to speak, to touch, to feed, to create. Those who lived in the time following the death and resurrection of Jesus went out and created something. They formed faith communities that changed the way they lived and ate and used their money. Though they believed that Jesus was coming back for them soon, they lived in such a

A number of musicians performed tonight, including a new female performer, Anna R. I am SO happy to see more women singing and being involved in the songwriting process at church. She gives me courage to forget about my fears and go for it. Anna and I are about to embark on some creative projects together—we will be doing a creative lesson trade. She will teach me modern dance, and I will give her piano lessons. Not using money seems like the most beautiful way to exchange or teach information about the arts. I am happy to invest in and pay to receive guitar and voice lessons, but it seems more Christian to just share what we have with each other. Anna and I also want to write a hymn-like song together. Our aim is to write a song way as to make their world more like God's Kingdom. Our calling is no different. We aid the Spirit in the work of the Kingdom by making all things better in our own time and place.

This understanding of the story entails that creativity is a central activity in the Kingdom of God. Imagine the Kingdom of God as the creative process of God reengaging in all that we know and experience. Imagine what it means to wonder if Jesus used so many metaphors for the Kingdom of God not because he couldn't find the right words, but because the Kingdom is like so many things, and so many things are like the Kingdom. When we employ creativity to make this world better, we participate with God in the re-creation of the world. And the habits and practices we acquire in the process of being co-(re)creators form us in the way of the life of God.

Our invitation to be involved in the work of God allows—maybe even commands—that we speak life, hope, beauty, and truth into all things. The gospel invites us into a future life—not only a future life after this one but also a future life during this one—in which we are to bless the world and make it better by creating in it. In the story of creation, Adam and Eve are called to make new people and to have dominion over all that is, to make it good and right. Similarly, our call to (re)creation is to make things the way they ought to be.

Imagine praying the Lord's Prayer this way:

> *Our Loving, Great Creator,*
> *Make the world different, the way you want it.*
> *Make this your place.*
> *Give to us in ways that we have not received before.*
> *Forgive us—make us new.*
> *Lead us into new good things and not into destruction.*

This is a prayer of the Kingdom. It is a prayer of creativity.

DUSTIN
Saturday

Defying all grown-up notions I sleep in until 11. After some leftover eggs and hashbrowns, I head off to get my hair cut. Every five weeks. I use my check-balancing program Quicken to tell me when it's time. Someday I hope to have a full-time girlfriend, or if I stumble on my bachelor's walk, a wife, who can act as a sort of personal stylist. See, I realize I have lots of . . . areas to

that not only rocks, but one that feels welcoming and familiar to new people, and that is in a singable key for women.

JAVIER
About 8 inches of snow fell last night, and while it was falling, Sarah and I went out and made a snowman on the front lawn of our apartment building. It was a lot of fun, and though it was my first snowman in my 28 years, I must say I did a marvelous job.

This was after a conversation I had with Luke this afternoon in which I suggested to him that we commission artists to create art that is specifically related to the biblical narrative.

Right now on the walls of our gathering space we have a potluck of different pieces from previous art lounges, intersections, and random additions.

I think that is fine as far as it goes, but I had a thought that maybe we should try to be more intentional with the things we are saying with the art in the gathering space. I didn't mean to imply that the art that is up right now doesn't say anything about the biblical narrative. I think that it does. I just started thinking that if we take such care in the way we use our language, then why should we not take the same care with our visual art?

3.3.2003
On Saturday night Sarah and I went to an art opening called "Skin" (http://www.iceboxminnesota.com/skinshow/skin-news.html). It is an exhibit revolving around the human body in art. It was an OK show. There were some really

improve, and one of the gaping holes is in personal style. If she could just make sure I don't wear something horrible out in public, I'd be grateful. Maybe we could even work it out where she sets out on the dresser what I'm going to wear the next day, and if she's going to be gone, she leaves a bunch of outfits in neatly stacked bags clearly labeled for the intended wear day. My last girlfriend taught me the importance of not wearing athletic socks everywhere and that just because it looks clean, doesn't mean it is clean.

But I imagine that would be a long ways away. I don't even like getting milk because it's a two-week commitment. I have three types of cereal in the cupboard so I can mix it up each morning. Shoot, I don't even like driving in the same lane for too long, let alone that whole "lifetime" holy bond by God stuff. Man . . .

Sunday

Again, the clock reads 10:49 as I attempt to climb out of my down comfort cocoon. I get the paper and a Diet Coke and read about the state's staggering deficit. I skim to find the arts budget slashed and curse at the "injustice." I'm sure my politics will change many times over the ages, but I'm currently in the supporting of the arts stage. I'm sure I'll move on to education and stuff as I grow older, maybe to return to this stage at an old age with money to toss around, but for now it gives me something to track. I voted in the last election based pretty much solely on what candidates had to say about the arts. Very little for most.

Thursday

I worked until 6:40 tonight and rushed home to watch the two-hour "Living with Michael Jackson" special on ABC. I skip working out or social contact to cocoon on the couch with some Chinese food and iced tea.

Wow. It was everything I'd dreamed it could be and so much more. There is nothing like feeling better about yourself at the expense of others. My life might be a bit weird or overwhelming from time to time, but man, I've got it so easy. I almost feel bad about skipping working out, but I know this will be all the talk at work tomorrow and anyone who is anyone will have an opinion. I mean really.

We hit the downtown movie complex. Tightly wedged between the Hard Rock Cafe and a GameWorks, it's a bit like going to a freaky carnival. Only without all the cool chained up animals.

Being ever time conscious, we buy our tickets early and head off to an Irish bar. On the way we hit Cold Stone Creamery for a little Oreo-on-Oreo ice cream action. Now, look at me and know I speak the truth when I say I have sampled ice cream the world over and this is some of the best. We go there at least twice a week during our lunch break. Or for creative inspiration. Or because it's Monday. Or Thursday. Never on earth has a more perfect union of milk and butter fat been achieved. Then to add double Oreos to the mix . . . sweet monkey, slow down I'm gett'n all hot and bothered.

Nothing follows up a good gorging on dairy like beer. We squeeze into one of the last empty booths by the door and comment on the crowd that just got out of a basketball game. Mar is hungry so we order a cheese tray. More dairy. Great.

IMAGINATIVE CHRISTIANITY

Art is creative, but creativity is not limited to art. People who do not understand themselves to be artists in the usual sense are also creative. At Solomon's Porch we make room in our personal and collective lives for creative activities of many sorts. Attending an art show in our gallery space or joining in a songwriting forum are creative activities, but so are leading the preschoolers in dancing and stories or brainstorming to help our Guatemala team raise money for the spring trip. What's important is living creatively and believing the world can be as God would have it.

Over the past few years I have tried to glean this sense of futurical vision from those in our community for whom creativity is as natural as the beating of the heart. They have shown me that faith without creativity can easily become faith without hope. Creativity breaks the bondage of what exists and frees us to frolic in the open spaces of what might be. Creativity moves us to participate—to join in the work of redemption rather than just watch it happen. Creativity gives us a sense of the future while bringing a here-and-now vibe to the activity of God. We begin to feel the things of God are happening in our time and place, not just in history. When the songs we sing or the words we read or the images we view were created just last week, we are reminded that the context of our faith is this moment and that we have something to bring into this life, right now.

I recognize that extending the activity of God into new areas is scary for some. There was concern when Abram was called into a new land to join in the creation of a new people. There was concern when the nation of Israel was to leave oppression and enter the land that was promised. There was serious apprehension when God's chosen people were told to live without a king.

And yet God met all these fears with creativity. What is the birth of a promised child to a barren woman but an act of creativity? The way the Messiah came into the world was a beautiful re-creation activity. It is foolish for those who would live in harmony with God to cling to the past while there is so much clear God activity happening in the world.

good pieces of work and some that lacked imagination and focus.

The interesting thing is that none of them were sexual in nature. I bet that would be surprising for staunch evangelical right-wing Republican Christians to hear, since most things that involve the human body and nudity are reserved for people like Larry Flynt or Hugh Hefner, shady parts of town, and their own private video collection.

I wonder sometimes what it would be like to create an "Intersection" at SP that deals with Song of Solomon. I think it would be a really good show, and it would be interesting to see how art speaks into the role of Christianity and sex.

It really is a shame that most people who see a nude think of it as primarily sensual. I *wonder if we as Christians began to redeem sex to what it was intended to be, would it free us to be able to enjoy the human body again? Not in some sensual sense, but in a genuine appreciation of the beauty of the human body.*

I wonder what people would say....

Every two months we have an art opening at Solomon's Porch – —an Art Lounge. This is a place where we give artists connected to Solomon's Porch an opportunity to have a show and display their work. The opening reception is much like any other you would find at most galleries. There are people milling around, looking at the work, interacting with the artist, listening to the music.

It is the night of the opening, and two months of

MAKING THINGS NEW

And so we have moved into our future with the idea that the Kingdom of God is synonymous with the creativity of God. We have sought to live our lives with imagination, cleverness, inventiveness, and ingenuity. A worship gathering at Solomon's Porch will often include bits of the familiar rhythms of more traditional worship. But it's important to us that elements of our gathering reflect the experiences of our community in our day.

Our worship gatherings almost feel like great improv—the band plays from memory, not from sheet music, and the sermon is created as it comes, not read from a written text. Someone may spontaneously share a brand-new poem or song. Communion is introduced by a different person each week, and there's no set script. Post-sermon discussions are free-form conversations with no agenda but to stay reasonably close to the subject at hand.

We never know quite where the night will go. And yet in this freedom, this sense of moving ahead without knowing exactly where God will move things, there is security as there is in the best kind of lovemaking: a time of finding new surprises in a comfortable place, of the deepest intimacy, of resting secure in the knowledge that our efforts will not be rejected.

We have found ourselves trying to figure out the most fitting ways to do particular things in our community. This applies to the arrangement of our space, our efforts of spiritual formation with children, our preaching, and our attempts to live as good neighbors. When we moved into our current space, there was a tremendous amount of remodeling needed to make the inside and outside of the building habitable. For three months people like Chris Dahn worked nearly every day tearing down and putting up walls. We painted and redesigned lighting. We planted new flowers, laid sod, and trimmed bushes. We would say to one another, "Here we go again, making the world better one building at a time." This served as a means of motivation, but also as a reflection of the belief that we join in the activity of God by making all things better.

SARAH

2.18.2003

Tonight I taught a class at the Edina Art Center. This is my second week. I've never taught before so it is very interesting. I get to plan curriculum and all that stuff so it's been very educational for me. I've heard that Doug is describing Javier and me as the "art couple." I don't really know what that is supposed to make us or how "artistic" we are supposed to be. I guess we have made a conscious effort to be creative and give creativity value; we strive to promote art in our surroundings and be people who encourage art. Why? I don't know if I can completely put it into words. It's just been something I've felt more internally and haven't felt the need to define. But I guess in order to communicate the feelings to others I should try to put words around it...

As I'm thinking of a way to write it, I'm coming across all the definitions of art that I've heard over my lifetime. "Anything creative," "it must be beautifully transcendent," or "the spiritual visually defined"... I'm still developing my philosophy of what I think art truly consists of.

Lately it's been on my mind that art isn't always creative or original. Not until the last one hundred years was art supposed to be something completely new and innovative: never been done before. People struggle to come up with a fantastic idea that has never been thought of before. It is no longer what the art is, rather what it's about. A urinal bought at a hardware store and placed in an art exhibition becomes a piece of art because it has an idea behind it... In the thousands of years that have come before these last hundred, art was rarely innovative or personal. As I walk through art museums I see the hundreds of pieces that we consider art from those past time periods. I think that there are two reasons they have lasted through the centuries for us to call them art: 1) Primarily they are records of history. They show us what was going on culturally and historically during certain time periods. Visual documentation of history, not necessarily solely the views of the individual artist. A majority of the pieces were commissioned by an organization or individual, not the original idea of the artist. 2) Quality and Skill. Those artists who are most highly regarded and whose pieces are still around are those who possessed amazing skill. A half-hearted effort just won't cut it.

FAILURE OF CREATIVITY

Our efforts at creativity almost always have an element of risk to them; there is an experimental feel. Our artists have led in creating this as an acceptable way to be. When art that comes from the deepest places of a person is hung on the wall for everyone to see, or something is performed with wide-eyed abandon, or a song is sung for the first time a message is being sent that it is permissible to step out, to generate something new, and to risk failing. There is seemingly no end to the things we have attempted that have not worked.

There are times when I become concerned that we make so many attempts that do not work that it becomes distracting to people.

From the start we wanted to reimagine the physical situation in our meeting space away from a front-facing, stage-focused approach. For the first two years we used a half-circle, moving to being fully in the round in our new, bigger space. Ben and I have had endless conversations about the struggles our setup

planning for this night culminate here.

I love those moments when faith, art, and life connect in the ways they were meant to. I wish they came along more often, and maybe they do come more often, and I just have to pay more attention.

It is those moments when faith and art both share equal leading duties that I love to help create.

The location of the gallery space is key, I think. Right now it is right next to the stairs that lead you to the gathering space. This means that every person who goes to a gathering walks by the gallery and is at least invited into the world of the artist.

So why is all this important to me? Why do I even bother to help champion the cause of art at Solomon's Porch? Because art helps us remember. It helps us to remember all the things that we wish we never would have, and maybe remind us of things that we should never forget. A good work of art does just that. It invites you to look inside of it, to explore it, to play inside it, and while you are in there, it is quietly and skillfully asking us to go back into the world changed. I don't think we can ever remain the same after experiencing good art.

So the Art Lounge is one of the ways that we try to achieve this—by inviting fellow artists to lead us into the places that we might not have gone ourselves or by helping us to notice the things we haven't taken the time to.

creates with sound, lighting, and sight lines. One day, in the midst of struggling with these and other issues that come with having a space that uses normal household furniture, Ben mused, "You know, maybe there are really good reasons people use stages." It was at this point that we intuitively knew we had a choice to make: we could give in to the tried and true convention or put a greater amount of creativity into play. With time and creativity we have worked out most of these issues and will most likely always meet in the round. (And who knows—maybe in a few decades someone in the midst of rearranging a worship space for the dozenth time will mutter, "You know, there were probably really good reasons people met in the round.")

Not all of our efforts have fared so well. When the church purchased a six-bedroom house in Minneapolis, the idea was that we'd have several people from our community live in the house as participants in an intentional community. It was an experiment in leadership development and community living. This effort failed in part because we hadn't thought it all out but also because failure is sometimes the result when you try something new. The decision to sell the house after 18 months wasn't the end of the world, but it was still painful for those of us who had invested time, dreams, and money into the project. We still believe the vision of a different kind of community formation is worth pursuing, though it may be some time before Solomon's Porch becomes a landlord again.

Still other creative efforts haven't turned out as we imagined. Our "Doxology"—a monthly time of prayer and communion with a lot of brilliant creative thinking behind it—never really became an essential part of our life as a community. We've held writing seminars and art exhibits that have been poorly attended. And as hard as we've worked to make our new space inviting—and despite all the incense we've burned—the building still has a funky smell that we just can't kill.

But the beauty of creativity as a means of spiritual formation is that even our "failures" breed hope. In most cases when a creative effort doesn't pan out, it's because the execution is flawed, not the dream. What matters isn't that we have the most beautiful flowers or the most atmospheric space or the most well-attended events. What matters is that all of these expressions are authentic outpourings from our community. We've learned that no matter how much confidence we have in a creative notion, there is always the chance that it might not work. That realization and our confidence that things will still be okay motivates us to risk putting our creative efforts on the table. Our confidence does not come from being successful at creativity; it comes from being certain that when we fail, things will be okay and we will continue to make things new.

There is, for some, an even greater risk involved in becoming co-(re)creators in the world. In the three years since Solomon's Porch became a reality, I've had more conversations than I can count about the emerging church and why it's seen as a threat to the evangelical way of life. Most often, the concern I hear is that the "postmodern" church has no sense of the Christian tradition, that it wants to scrap everything that's come before it and make something new. Maybe that's true in some churches that call themselves "postmodern." But what I've seen in the emerging, post-industrial church is a desire not to ignore what's come before us, but to be informed and inspired by it as we create ways of living in harmony with God in our time. The great risk of the church is not in losing our traditions; it is losing our ability to reimagine. I really don't know what to do with the approach to faith that tells us all the answers have been discovered and we are simply to apply those answers to our lives. I don't know how we are supposed to worship with songs, prayers, and confessions created for other times and places. And I really don't know how to live out an understanding of the gospel that says I don't have a part to play in what God is doing in the world. Creativity is at the center of God's image. It is how we see God and talk to God and find our hope in God. I can't figure out any other way to respond to God's (re)creation of the world, to God's invitation that we join in as co-(re)creators, than to live as creative people.

So the night ends, and everyone goes home. Sarah and I talk about the evening on the drive home, happy with the turnout but always hoping that more people from Solomon's Porch would have shown up. There is always the next time, we say, and the planning for the next Art Lounge starts tomorrow.

On the Rise

I've been thinkin'
About a dream.
I hope you'll join me,
Where forming means
Are unfolding and it seems
To me...

That you've been thinkin'
About a dream.
And you've got a reason
To believe
And I'm hoping that we see...

Chorus:
That we've arrived by fountain
Been pursued through the sky.
And in times of renouncement
What was dead is on the rise.

Those who stood beneath Him
Heard Him breathe.
And suppose we had only
Heard Him scream, "It is finished."
So it seemed,
But He...

Givin' faith to my dreams
And death has lost its sting.
My life will ever be awakened.
"And when from death I'm free
I will sing on"
Wholly reconciled.

"And when from death we're free
we will sing on
and through eternity we will sing on."

CHAPTER 09

SPIRITUAL FORMATION THROUGH SERVICE

SATURDAY

Let me set the scene for you. My name is Kathryn Prill. I was on staff with Solomon's Porch for the first three years of its life. In January 2003 I escaped my life and moved to Guatemala for a few months. The previous spring I had been a part of Solomon's Porch's annual trip to build houses in a small village. As soon as I returned to the States, I began to make plans to return. Eight months later, I was back in Guatemala. At the time of which I write, I was in the middle of a three-week study. After Spanish school, I would travel to the city with which Solomon's Porch has a relationship, San Juan La Laguna.

I was studying Spanish in a school in the western city of Quetzaltenango, or Xelá (pronounced Shey-la) for short. The central park square of Xelá is full at all hours with roll-away store carts, students, entertainers, and homeless people. Some of the most persistent characters in the square are the shoe-shine boys. They are all 12 years old or younger and always filthy.

I became deft at rebuffing the shoe-shiners, although I never really liked saying no. Solomon's Porch fosters the Christian senses of mercy and justice, and refusing a poor, dirty child, no matter how annoying or inappropriate his offered service, always felt horrible.

When the next boy came around and asked to shine my shoes, I was wearing running shoes. I explained to him that they weren't the kind of shoes that get shined, but I'd like it if he sat down and talked to me. He did, even though he made it clear that he was in the park to work. His name was Pedro, and he was nine years old. He lived a mile or so from the park square and didn't attend school. He had five brothers and sisters, including a baby brother. He didn't know his dad. His mom couldn't work because of all the kids, and Pedro needed to make any money he could to help his family.

ERIN

I woke up in a great mood after some dreams about Guatemala. I dreamed that I was there, that it was beautiful. In my dream I didn't want to build houses at all, wanted to play outside and be in the water. The locals and my friends all scolded me and told me that I should be working harder. I have been pondering going to Guatemala in August, so this dream compels me to inquire more about the trip and the work that would be involved.

2 June, 2003
Katherine and James and I started developing a dream tonight. We realized how much we would like to share our gifts with the community in Guatemala and develop a healing camp. Our clinic would provide free massage, chiropractic, and bioresonance treatments

A shoe shine was out of the question, so I asked Pedro if he would like something from the McDonald's near the park. His eyes lit up. "¿Caja Feliz?" he exclaimed—that's Spanish for "Happy Meal."

When we reached the benches at the perimeter of the park, Pedro sat down and told me he would wait there. McDonald's has an armed guard outside its doors, and one of his functions is to keep out street kids like Pedro. I sighed and made Pedro promise to wait right there.

I confess to feeling like the newly crowned Social Service Queen of Latin America as I went into McDonald's. I should have known better, but the fullness of the moment blinded me to what I know about the way God works. I fully believe that God's favorite device is irony, and in a few minutes God would remind me of that.

I had forgotten completely that Happy Meals come with a small toy. This one was a plastic Snoopy. It didn't fit in the box along with the food, so I slipped it into my bag.

As I doled out the cheeseburger, the fries, the soda, Pedro's face remained impassive. I wondered what I could do to get the reaction I was looking for. Then I remembered.

"And look, Pedro, a Snoopy toy!" I pulled the doll out of my bag and handed it to him.

Then, and only then, he smiled.

That was a defining moment for me, both in my trip and within my life. For all my posturing and pride in buying Pedro his meal, it was neither me nor the food I provided that brought him joy.

No: I was trumped by a plastic Snoopy.

Every time I tell this story, I relive the look on Pedro's face and the feeling in my crushed heart. I am reminded that no matter how great I think I am, no matter how proud I am of myself for following Jesus in the way I see fit, no matter how many miles I am from home, God is right there with me, reminding me what it means to serve. In that moment, in seeing unbrushed teeth sparkle in the presence of plastic Snoopy, I saw that service doesn't have to be bought. The blessing is that God works through us— through our pride, through our money, through whatever lame earthly goal we have in mind. The way of the Kingdom is not the way of this world.

I took Pedro's smile and lesson with me for the rest of my weeks in Guatemala. I was careful when sharing my bounty of goods, but tried to give in the spirit abundantly. I kept looking for God every hour I was there, and I was pleasantly surprised to continually discover God was there. Whether in the form of a child's dirty hands patting my white skin or in the joy of having my friends land on the beach of San Juan on the final Saturday of my trip—serving me, forming me, and leading me to do the same. I spent the majority of my time in San Juan. Solomon's Porch has included them in our community for four years now; our members make the trek down there every spring and fall to build homes for some of the poorest people in the village, and since 2002, we as a church have maintained a presence there. In the fall of 2002, Shana Andersen included San Juan in her four-month stay in Guatemala. I was the winter 2003 edition, and after the Porch's trip in the spring of 2003, Dustin Smith stayed on in San Juan for three weeks.

We live there not to provide a service (remember: you will be trumped by a plastic toy) but to continue to build friendships within the body of Christ. It is truly a friendship and not just glorified visiting. All the Porchers who go to San Juan are asked for updates on the absent. It was a great honor to be welcomed by people I had never met as Shana's friend, as Anna's friend, as a friend of Timoteo and Douglas El Gigante, as una miembra del Portico de Solomon. And I am so blessed, as are many others of Solomon's Porch, to call many of the Guatemaltecos of San Juan La Laguna my friends.

If we are not the company we keep—whether it's Jesus or simply our friends on earth—who are we?

...

WHO ARE OUR NEIGHBORS?

From the beginning, life with God has been about service. The teachings of Jesus are suffused with the invitation to be a people who love and serve our neighbors.

Now there's nothing new in that. There's nothing original about sending people to build houses in Guatemala, giving money to people in need, or believing that serving others is an essential component of walking in the way of Jesus. We know we are not doing something new by making service a practice of our spiritual formation. We are not bushwhacking our way into new territory with some

for several weeks annually to our Guatemalan friends. By night, we would love to teach yoga and healthy-cooking classes.

4 June, 2003
Tonight was a very poignant example of the generosity of the people of Solomon's Porch. Tonight we fashioned our typical women's event night into a shower for a new family in our community. Mindy and her girls have been coming to church for a few months, and when they came, they had little except obedience to God and a willingness to trust. It has been wonderful to watch this family make themselves at home at church and to see how God has provided for them. Many people have been very helpful to this family over the last few months, but people gave overwhelmingly to this family tonight.

In her own words, Mindy went from having nothing to having more than she needs. It was beautiful to see how graciously she accepted help and to see that many of the women who had needs themselves—single mothers, students, stay-at-home mothers—made room for Mindy and their girls in their hearts and in their pocketbooks.

DUSTIN

The Porch has made it a biyearly event to send a group down to Guatemala to build houses and such in a community we've "adopted." I don't really like the word adopted, because it implies that we are much wiser and must nurture the common man. On the contrary, I think that we both have a lot to learn from each other, and much of the time people come home with a sense that

novel expression of Christianity; we are trying to ride along the rails of the well-established faith of those who have gone before us. And frankly, that's fine. Our motivation for serving others is not to be unique or hip.

We're committed to living lives of service because of its formative qualities. Service isn't how we act out our spirituality; it's how our spirituality gets shaped. And as such, it's not reserved for the elite of the faith.

In the early days of Solomon's Porch we were captured by this verse from the book of James:

Religion that God our Father accepts as pure and faultless is this: to look after orphans and widows in their distress and to keep oneself from being polluted by the world. (James 1:27)

We were enraptured by this call not as a way to live out our faith but as a means into our faith. As part of our spiritual formation we wanted to answer that call and be useful religious people. We were then, and are still, quite sure that the world is not made better by more people having the I-am-not-religious, I-have-a-relationship-with-God attitude. Rather, the world needs people who are living religiously useful lives in and for the world. We want to be that kind of people, and we know this means making service a normal practice of our spiritual formation. Living in the way of Jesus is not a result of a deeper devotion to the things of Jesus; it is what develops in us that deeper devotion.

Service is an obvious way for us to orient our lives around both a belief in Jesus and our efforts to live in the Kingdom of God and never separate the two or pit them against each other.

One of the ways we describe Solomon's Porch is as a holistic missional Christian community. It is a phrase that people read with interest and a bit of confusion ("Is *missional* really a word?" Yes, it's the adjectival form of the word *mission*.) One advantage to using a peculiar phrase is that it makes people stop and think about what we're up to.

But there's more to it than a desire to be provocative. To say we are a missional community is to say that we are not the end users of the gospel—our belief in God and our living in the way of Jesus are not for our benefit alone. Rather we receive these so that we may be equipped and sent into the world to love our neighbors and serve "the least of these." In this sense, Solomon's Porch doesn't have a mission; it is missional.

SHAPED BY SERVICE

It's tempting to see service primarily as a way for the well-resourced to reach out to others. But that perspective makes service a kind of condescension—drops of mercy bestowed upon the "needy" by those who are "blessed"—rather than an outgrowth of our desire to work toward making things on earth as they are in Heaven.

Carol, a single mother with an eight-year-old son, lived in a house owned and subsidized by our church. When the time came for us to sell the house, members of our community used their connections with apartment managers, social workers, housing authorities, and job training services to help Carol and Donald find a safe, affordable place to live. What was clear during this process is that no one thought of Carol as a project. This wasn't a veiled program attempt to make her a better Christian, although we recognize that our efforts contributed to Carol's understanding of the life of faith.

Of course we recognize that people are poor in a variety of ways, and that the poor in spirit need the help of others as surely as those who are just plain poor. We have helped people in our community pay the rent, find a therapist, find a job, get medication, heal a marriage, deal with divorce, treat depression, find safe housing, and more—and none of this has come through a structured program. We aren't trying to be missionaries, but friends who love and serve one another when there is a need.

The process of helping Carol find a home, helping an unemployed mother get some furniture, or lending the van to a family with young children benefits others as it changes our community. When we participate in acts of service, we are stretching our faith to make sure it fits the world we live in. If our faith can't move us to feed someone who is hungry or help a single mother find shelter, it's simply not useful in the world.

Our yearning to be a people who love and bless the world means we understand that service extends beyond our threshold; we seek to care for those outside our immediate community with the same compassion. As I'll show later, this way of living isn't an outgrowth of faith but rather the essential means to our spiritual formation.

they gave us more than we could have ever given them.

I had no doubt that the trip would be a life-changing event for me, but I just don't feel like I have had the calling to go yet. First off, I really have a tough time getting over the fundraising aspect of it. I don't feel like I'm in the position to send out hundreds of letters to friends and family to say, "Hey, I'm off to build houses, how much do you love God?" That's drastic, but I have reservations nonetheless.

Plus, I'm sure there are other more qualified people to go. Stronger builders or more friendly teachers. I'd be the gringo who sat in the shade all day throwing sticks for the kids to fetch and thinking of ways to smuggle Cuban cigars back into the country.

I once roughed it in the wild for a week, and by the end I thought I was going to die. It turns out I was just in a Holiday Inn in Des Moines.

JIM

11/02

Instead of debating academically over whether or not this war is "just," it seems that we at SP ought to take seriously the question, "How ought we to practice peacemaking among ourselves and in our community on a regular basis?" Is not the best we have to offer the world an example that we are a community who is at peace among ourselves and our immediate neighbors? How could we put this peacemaking to practice? The best I can imagine is an SP community that is vitally connected with one another; one in which we practice service and forgiveness to

THE NEIGHBORHOOD

The gospel commands us to love our neighbors, not to be market-driven. At Solomon's Porch we try not to see our church as a means of meeting needs in order to convince people that the gospel is attractive. Our role in the world should not be limited to teaching about God or filling the felt needs of an ever-desiring culture; instead we should love God and our neighbors without having ulterior motives for either of them. We are trying to be good neighbors who are formed by the love of God and invite others into that process.

In our current neighborhood, two-thirds of our neighbors don't speak English as their first language. This means they're not terribly likely to attend our worship gatherings, but it doesn't mean they're any less our neighbors. We are still called to love them as neighbors. The question we faced when we moved into our neighborhood was...how?

We had very few models to look to. Many churches start in poor urban centers and stay there or start in poor urban centers and then move into desirable neighborhoods. But not many young, thriving churches move from desirable neighborhoods into poor urban centers. Much of how we're trying to live in this neighborhood is the result of trial and error.

As a community we had no interest in posturing as "urban commando Christians" doing the hard work of faith with the poor and needy. For one thing, we did not target our neighborhood; circumstances, size, price, and availability made this the clear choice for us. Moving into the city core was not seizing a higher calling. It was the situation God orchestrated for us, and we wanted to live into it. For another thing, we never set out to "save the neighborhood" or "bring light to this dark place." That attitude feels a little racist and patronizing. It's also dead wrong. The neighborhood boasts as high a level of social services as any in the country; more to the point, there are many churches. We were not bringing in that which was missing–we were invited to be the newest participants in the Kingdom of God as it unfolds on 13th Avenue.

Bob Brantly is a neighbor who coordinates a prayer ministry for the neighborhood. Not long after Solomon's Porch moved in, he sent me this e-mail:

Dear Pastor Pagitt,

I am with the Phillips Prayer Group, a multicultural, nondenominational group that meets each Friday from 7 to 8 a.m. at Oliver Presbyterian Church (27th and Bloomington) to pray for the pastors, churches, min-

istries, and needs of the neighborhood. We pray regularly for unity in the Body, reconciliation of all kinds, and the winning of souls for Christ. We have been at it now for nine years and have seen some marvelous answers to our prayers. We believe the presence of Solomon's Porch in the neighborhood is one of these answers, and we welcome you with all our hearts.

You are already listed on our prayer request list for tomorrow, but if you receive this in time and let me know your prayer needs, we can make it more specific. You are also cordially invited to join us tomorrow morning, or whenever it is convenient, and become either a regular or occasional member of the group.

Finally, I would like to invite you to join me–and another pastor, Darrell Geddes, senior pastor of Christ's Church International–for lunch on Monday, Aug. 26, which would afford us an opportunity to get acquainted.

Again, how good it is to have you in the neighborhood. I look forward to your reply.

Yours in Christ, Bob Brantly

Obviously we at Solomon's Porch were not in this on our own, then or now.

The best way to be a good neighbor for the first year, we decided, was not to do formal outreach. We concentrated on being friendly. We held an open house so we could meet the neighbors and they could meet us. We invited people to join us for Sunday-afternoon cookouts, and we welcomed their children to garden with us. During the course of the year we met people from the neighborhood, and many joined us in all kinds of Kingdom of God efforts, so it wasn't exactly a stagnant year for our ministry–but it was also healing for us not to have to create a series of programs to justify our presence. In any case, whether it's the free cookouts or our penchant for keeping the front of the entire building clean and well-groomed or something else, people seem to be as glad to have us as neighbors as we are to be there.

After that first year it made sense to be more deliberate with our presence on the block. But even then we didn't do research to see what the neighborhood needed and then create programs and hire experts to meet those needs. Then as now, we look instead at what we all have to offer–ideas, passions, resources,

one another, and a community which seeks ways to invite others in our community into friendship with us. This seems so idealistic, but I don't think it is—we experience this kind of community in our covenant group. Would it not be worthwhile to intentionally, as an entire SP community, get together over food with a local Muslim congregation? Or to worship with our Christian church neighbors? Would it not be peacemaking to have regular "good neighbor" meals by inviting our community into our doors for food and friendship?

It seems that peacemaking now—right here among ourselves and our community—will be the leaven of God's Kingdom that will make violence unthinkable between us at SP and all who meet us in times of future conflict. Imagine that; a church that refuses to do violence to a people it has come to know and love. God save us.

SARAH

3/24

I think Javier's car may be dead for good. It needs a new carburetor, and believe me, it's not worth paying to replace the part. Javier sent a little message out in the weekly e-mail to see if anyone was selling a car cheaply. What do you know, Erin (a fellow blogger) sent an e-mail back saying she was selling a car. It sounds like a great deal, and she's going to bring it by tomorrow evening for us to look at. She's even going to let us make payments to her so we don't have to get a loan. That's such a blessing because we have so many other financial issues we're deal-

abilities—that could further the reconciliation work of the Kingdom. Serving our neighbors thus looks less like a sophisticated social-service program than like a guy lending out his lawn mower. Here are some examples.

- We utilize a high-speed computer modem for our church work, and for very little cost we were able to network other computers to create an Internet café that's available to our neighbors at no cost.

- Our facility houses a tutoring program for elementary-age children, a group that teaches English to adult Somalis, a church that meets on Saturday nights, and a program that helps teenagers develop personal and job skills by making T-shirts. We are restructuring part of our facility so neighborhood friends can use our washer and dryer. In addition, our people who love children and are gifted at running camps offer a series of summer day camps with an emphasis on sports, art, and creativity.

- Being good neighbors did not start with our move to our new location. In Linden Hills, where the needs are not necessarily financial or physical in nature, we helped staff a neighborhood festival, regularly walked around the nearby lake to pick up garbage, and ran an afternoon story time for children during the summer.

Living as good neighbors is not always easy. In our neighborhood the language barrier can be difficult to negotiate. There's also a natural fear of getting sucked into hard situations. (Remember the drug-dealing car on Tuesday night?) But when we take the step and engage our lives with those around us and find ourselves not only thinking like Jesus but living like Jesus, there is a transformation that is unlike anything else. That is spiritual formation at its best.

Sometimes that spiritual formation requires us to define "neighborhood" even more broadly. We took a group to Guatemala for a home-building trip during our first year as a church. It wasn't that we had a supply of "mature Christians" who were ready for the next level of discipleship. In fact, what we had were not-yet-mature Christians who were in need of the kind of formation that can only happen in service to others—and that happens especially transformationally in an immersion situation. With our connections I knew we could create an atmosphere that would encourage this formation to take place. Even better, we could develop a long-term partnership with friends whom we could visit year after year. Our Guatemalan Christian family would serve us by giving abundantly out of their poverty and teaching us how to live in the way of Jesus, at least as much as we served them. And so it has turned out.

Even the kind of stomach illness that accompanied many trips to Central America has a role in spiritual transformation. Sharing the ongoing digestive irregularity of our new friends in Guatemala would create in us a rudimentary solidarity with the poor that would not allow us to stay as we were in our spiritual formation.

As our relationship with the village of San Juan has evolved through four trips and constructing more than 20 homes, it is clearer to me than ever that efforts like these are not the specialized dessert of spiritual formation but the main course.

21ST-CENTURY NEIGHBORS?

Jesus told the parable of the Good Samaritan to teach that our neighbor is anyone in our world who needs our help.

In Jesus' day the world that a follower was called to care for was really quite small, bounded perhaps by the distance that she could walk in a day. She may never have traveled more than 100 miles from home—in fact, Jesus probably never made it that far. She wouldn't have been concerned about people 10,000 miles away because she wouldn't have known they even existed.

But I do know they're there. Stories of what is happening around the world are more accessible than the stories from our very own neighborhood. It is not at all unusual for me to know details about what's going on in the Gaza Strip before I know what's happening on Lake Street, even while I'm driving on Lake Street.

And that fundamentally changes how I understand the answer to "Who is my neighbor?" I can go to bed every night knowing about people all over the world for whom I am doing nothing. It's almost overwhelming to live out the call of Jesus to love our neighbor as ourselves when the world is our neighbor.

But I am called, and we are called, to try.

Because we understand that the gospel is not for us alone but for the the whole world, we can't avoid asking, "What am I going to do about AIDS in Africa, war in the Middle East, and homelessness in Central America?" The work of God in the world is no longer reserved for long-term missionaries or Christian leaders. Today regular people like us—artists and mothers and computer programmers—can build housing developments and hospitals in Guatemala. We can arrange for

ing with—IRS, credit cards, college loans…it seems like we get something under control and something else happens—like having to find money for a car. The thing is, I never expected to find something so good at a reasonable price that we could make payments on. And the best part is that the money from this book and a couple other free-lance ventures should pay for most of it. God is good. He provides in the most amazing ways.

JAVIER
1.29.2003
Here I am at work trying to think through what I need to do today and quite proud that I am doing this right now instead of later on in the day when inevitably I will be distracted by guys talking to me about all their problems.

I guess I really haven't made it clear that I work at a chemical dependency treatment facility. I am the Learning Center Coordinator there, and my responsibilities are to oversee the education component of the treatment program. Guys come in here after they are in the program for one month and begin to learn basic computer skills, and, if they need it, we help them get ready to take their GED test. And for the ones who need help with their literacy we set them up with tutors to help them with their reading and writing. On Wednesday afternoons I teach a life skills class made up of 12 modules that deal with major issues most guys here face. They range from dealing with today's class to making right decisions to effective listening skills. It is

food to feed an entire village in Eritrea. We can work to free slaves in places we never heard of. There are few, if any, excuses not to listen to our call to serve our global neighborhood.

As one of our dreams puts it (see p. 17), our desire is to be a people who "are connected to, dependent on, and serve the global Church." So we give resources to people in our community who travel to other parts of the world, we fund AIDS orphans in India and Africa, and we're checking into ministry opportunities in Jamaica, Africa, China, Iraq, and Afghanistan. People may wonder why we are so involved around the world when there is so much need in our own country. Our answer is simple: The community of God is not restricted by national allegiance. We are no less obligated to people who live in a foreign country than we are to people who live inside our borders.

How we care for the needy in the world is not often clear, and our efforts so far have been very limited. But we are quite sure that our faith must play out globally as well as locally and that our formation as people living in harmony with God depends on it.

A TECHNOLOGICAL ANSWER?

In the late 1990s I was part of a pastors' event that was held at Apple Computer headquarters. One of the presenters announced excitedly that, within a decade, technology would make it possible to communicate the gospel all around the world, even the most remote areas, without having to travel there.

Digitize the gospel beyond all face-to-face contact? That misses the point. The incarnation was not God's stopgap until we humans could develop better technology. There is no avoiding the role that relational flesh-on-flesh servanthood played in the earthly ministry of Jesus. And there is no avoiding it in our lives, either.

At a Sunday-night worship gathering awhile back, Steve asked for help for a family he had recently met. He had been at a youth camp during the week and had met a boy whose family was struggling. The boy desperately wished his family would keep the house clean. When camp ended, Steve took this boy home—and discovered that the house was not merely messy: Earlier in the week the health department had condemned it as unlivable. If the house wasn't set right so the family could move back in, the boy and his siblings could end up in the custody of the state. That night our community agreed to help clean the house.

It turns out that the family is involved with a church that was unaware of the situation. We arranged to clean the house so people of the other church could spend time getting help for the family in other areas, notably the underlying psychological issues. The next week there were people from our community in that house every day filling dumpster after dumpster with decades-old items, rotten food, dead animals, and rancid carpet. The stench was so bad everyone had to wear face coverings.

At last report, the family is falling back into its old ways. That's disappointing, of course. But for the people of Solomon's Porch who went to that house and cleared out the garbage of strangers, not for pay or out of professional obligation but because they know that living their lives to love and care for those in need is a part of becoming like Jesus, it was a holy week. And if going back to that house in those conditions is what it takes to make that family's world better, I am sure many from our community will be donning face masks again.

one of my favorite times of the week because the way I have the class set up is more of a discussion-based thing, because the residents here get preached at way too much.

3.5.2003
I wonder what it would be like if becoming a follower of Christ meant no blessings or good things coming into your life. I wonder because here where I work there are a lot of people on staff and residents who sincerely believe in that whole "prosperity gospel" stuff. They go to the churches, quote the preachers, buy the books—they do it all. It gets maddening at times, and it is always nauseating. The whole idea that God blesses you with stuff or that you are entitled to material and monetary blessings just because you are a follower of his repulses me.

Every fiber of my being cringes at the thought that there are tons of people wanting to follow God, and some idiot preacher comes along and feeds them the prosperity message. My conclusion is that it is neither the gospel nor good news, at least not to the poor who follow God and still struggle to pay bills. It sure isn't good news to the millions of Christians in developing countries who have learned through true persecution, or seeing part of their body martyred, what it means to follow God. I would guess that if God were going to bless anyone with stuff and money, he would choose the poor people and not the richest group of Christian suburbanites the world has ever known. You ask them why this "gospel" isn't seen all over the world,

Made

*You keep asking me to follow,
Leave this sanity,
Of a way we can't even swallow;
A people we call free.
But they're not so free, not so free,
'Cause all I see is a people in chains.*

*"Join the rat race,"
"Make your mom proud,"
"Put on your game face,"
If it's not too loud,
Enjoy the sound of "American made,"
But that's not how we're made,
Not to make things for ourselves,
But to be*

*Made
Unto You,
To learn to be free
How we're intended to be.
Made
Unto Your Son,
To love one another and not just be loved.*

*I keep wondering,
Am I of any use,
Am I leaving a legacy?
But the steps I take that are nearer to the truth,
Are the steps leading away from me.
'Cause it's not about me,
Not about me, not about my image
Of pedestals made of clay,
It's when we realize that it's all about You,
That's when we,
That's when we are*

*Made,
Unto You*

Until we learn to be free,
How we were intended to be.
Made.
Unto to Your Son,
To love one another and not just be loved.
I wanna be made…

and all they do is give you that deer-in-the-headlights look.

It would be pretty funny if it weren't so sad.

CHAPTER 10

EXPERIMENTATION AND THE LONG HAUL

GOING FORTH

Well, that's a week at Solomon's Porch.

At our Sunday-night worship gathering you sank into one of our couches and learned how and why we make the worship interactive and holistic.

You came to yoga class on Monday night and encountered our respect for the physical dimensions of worship and life in Jesus.

On Tuesday you joined us for the Bible discussion group that shapes our sermon and experienced how we share teaching authority in dialogue.

You experienced our hospitality at the Wednesday-night dinner and heard how that is a part of Kingdom living.

On Thursday you came along to Bible study and saw how Solomon's Porch handles belief formation: like a tango of information and hope and experience and grace.

On Friday you walked through a Way of the Cross to which Porchers young and old had contributed with their creativity.

On Saturday you mulled over service with our community, our neighbors, and the world, and you saw how sweat and caring and even a plastic Snoopy bring us to a place of useful faith.

And now, as we cycle back to Sunday, I hope you've gotten a sense of Solomon's Porch as a community in which people who don't have all the answers take risks and make mistakes in the course of living into the call of Kingdom life together.

What we're about, as I said at the beginning, is moving beyond education as the primary form of spiritual formation. Not surprisingly, some people have pointed questions: They wonder whether what we're doing is a trendy reaction against the church that will experience its own backlash in time, or they want to know whether what we are doing is viable financially or in areas of church growth.

My answer? "I don't know, and it really doesn't matter that much to me."

I am increasingly convinced that what matters in our efforts is our willingness to experiment and try—to develop expressions of faith that are fully of our day and time, recognizing that our efforts will be adapted and changed in years to come. Our role is to do our part in our day and time. It's not important to me whether someone is still singing our songs or using our couches 15 years from now (my hope is that they will sing their own songs and figure out their own seating). It's the spirit of exploring, of seeking, of risking that I hope will inspire future generations. Our duty to those who follow is to leave a legacy of faith and not particular programs. While being led by the broader community of faith, including those who have come before us, we need to be people of the future—people whose ways of spiritual formation and life with God can flex and grow to meet the needs of our changing world. This adaptability is taken for granted in our means of communication, modes of transportation, medical practices, and even our wardrobe. How much more important it is in developing our faith!

People sometimes get tripped up on this idea of thinking ahead and being fully engaged in our culture, because it sounds like I'm suggesting that we let the culture shape the church, which raises the "slippery slope" flag for some.

To rely solely on the past for our ideas about spiritual formation is simply not consistent with the call of the Kingdom of God. How so? Let me explain it like this.

My wife and I recently had a conversation about buying furniture for our home. We don't want to spend an excessive amount of money, but more importantly, we want products as good as the antiques we own. I mentioned to Shelley that I get tired of hearing people moaning that furniture makers don't make well-crafted furniture anymore. I simply don't think that's true. There is as much high-quality furniture today as ever—but now it seems too expensive because we have more access to cheaper products than during previous times. We could work with a craftsman and purchase a rocker or an armoire that will last for generations, but it will cost us. It's hard to swallow the expense when we know we could buy a nice-enough knockoff version for a fraction of the price. So the struggle is not in finding good, quality furniture–it's being willing to pay for it. I asked Shelley if we should be the kind of people who purchase high-quality goods that our grandchildren will revere, or are we going to be the kind who only live off the quality of generations gone by, and buy cheap stuff made during our time? A similar question confronts communities of faith. Will we do the hard and costly work of hand-crafting faith in our day, or will we be content living off the antiques of previous generations and fill in with cheap imitations of our own to "freshen up" the old stuff? Are we willing to become artisans of new expressions of faith so that our grandchildren will see as their legacy the quality that came before them, so they will be stirred thereby to craft newer, more beautiful, more meaningful expressions in their own day?

This book is primarily about one community and the practices of spiritual formation in it. But the creativity required to live an imaginative, experimental faith is not limited to what we do during our worship gatherings or Wednesday night dinners. Central to the types of spiritual formation discussed in this book is the need for us—not only our Solomon's Porch community but the church as a whole—to become theological communities.

The work of theology must happen in full community. Of course it must include the ideas of those who have come before us, but to simply accept the work of our forebears in the faith as the end of the conversation is to outsource the real work of thinking, and that turns theology into a stagnant philosophy rather than an active pursuit of how we are to live God's story in our time. The communities that are best equipped for the task of spiritual formation in the post-industrial age are those who make the practice of theology an essential element of their lives together. This is in no way a call to be less theological, but a call to our communities to be more involved in the work of theology as a necessary part of the spiritual formation process.

Wouldn't it be wonderful if the task of both the new convert to Christianity and the experienced Christian was understood as not only believing the things of Christianity, but also as contextualizing, creating, articulating, and living the expressions of faith in their world? New Testament Christians lived it with the debate about how non-Jews would be called to live as followers of Jesus. The early Christians ultimately were called to a kind of spiritual formation that allowed Gentiles to fully follow Jesus in ways that were culturally appropriate to Gentiles. I am confident that we too will gradually move beyond the pre-industrialized approach of spiritual formation to one that better fits our own time.

Similarly, Abram was called by God into new lands and new ways of living. We are invited to live a faith like Abram's, and like him to be radically committed to an unknown future that does not rest in finding new ways to do the same old things but in finding new ways to do the new things of Jesus in our time. We can sustain that commitment only with the faith that God goes with us and that the Holy Spirit serves as our teacher and guide.

And now, as a week ends and another begins, it's time to go forth.

Our worship gathering ends each Sunday with a blessing we sing to one another as we prepare to take our faith out into the world. Let me leave with you one of the blessings; of the songs we use regularly, it's the only one that is not original with us. Perhaps you already know it.

Irish Blessing

May the road rise up to meet you,
May the wind be always at your back,
May the sun shine warm upon your face,
And the rains fall soft upon your fields.
And until we meet again, my friend
Until we meet again
May God hold you in the palm of His hand.

And may you be blessed on your journey of Spirit-filled, imaginative, 21st-century Christian faith and life.

PHOTO CREDITS

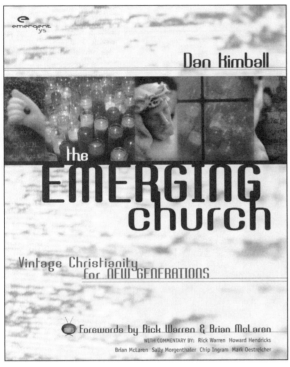

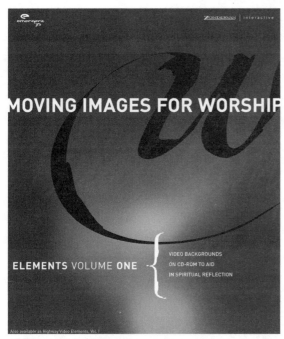
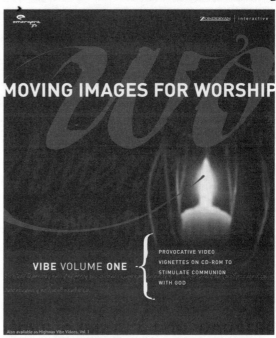

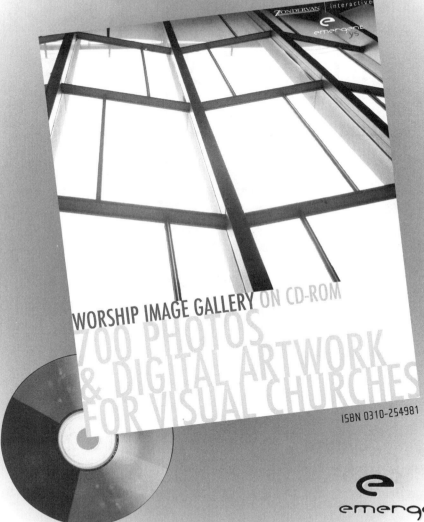

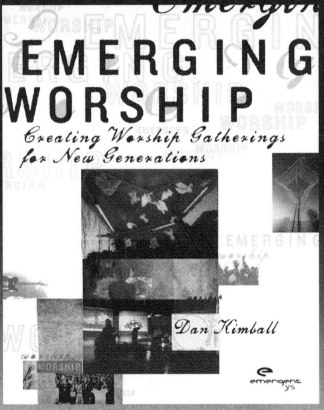